Editor
MARYANNE BLACKER
Designer
ROBBYLEE PHELAN
Assistant Editor
JUDY NEWMAN
Cadet Artist
LOUISE MCGEACHIE
Secretary
WENDY MOORE

Photographer
ESTHER BEATON

Consultants
JAN GREGG
ANNE RATTY
SONIA WILLIAMS
JUDY REIZES

Design Director
NEIL CARLYLE
Editor-in-Chief
SANDRA FUNNELL
Publisher
RICHARD WALSH

Creative play enhances not only artistic development but also self esteem, decision making skills, creative thinking, and appreciation of others as individuals. We've gathered the most educational, effective and enjoyable activities for our second Children's Art and Crafts book. It's a helpful resource for parents, carers, teachers, playgroup organisers and others who work with children. Use the pictures in this book as a guide; encourage children to experiment and create, rather than copy. And keep in mind that the value of a child's art lies in the "doing", not the end result.

Produced by The Australian Women's Weekly
Home Library.
Typeset by Letter Perfect, Sydney.
Printed by Dai Nippon Co Ltd, Tokyo, Japan.

Published by Australian Consolidated Press,
54 Park Street, Sydney.
Distributed in the U.K. by Australian Consolidated
Press (U.K.) Ltd (0604) 760 456. Distributed in New
Zealand by Gordon and Gotch (N.Z.) Ltd
(09) 654 397. Distributed in Canada by Whitecap
Books Ltd (604) 980 9852. Distributed in South
Africa by Intermag (011) 493 3200.

More Children's Art & Crafts.
  Includes index.
  ISBN 0 949892 72 6.
  1. Handicraft. 2. Creative activities and seat work.
  (Series: Australian Women's Weekly Home Library).
745.5083

*Our thanks to the staff and students of North
Sydney Leisure Centre, NSW, who provided
the location for photography and made the
majority of the projects featured in this book.*

Contents

Guidelines
2
Painting
4
Printing
22
Dyeing
38
Touch and Feel
46
Construction and Collage
56
Masks and Hats
66
Weaving and Stitching
78
Puppets
88
Recycled Fun
106
Index
128

Guidelines

The following information is intended as a helpful guide for families, preschools, child carers and kindergartens when setting up a collection of art and craft equipment. Some materials used in our projects are explained and suggestions are given for other useful materials to collect.

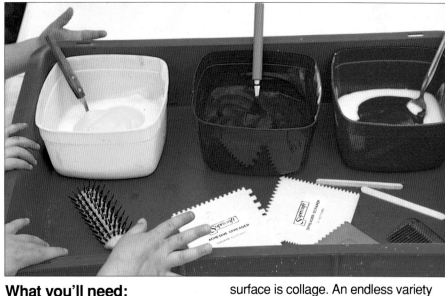

OVER 2 YEARS

AGE: The ages given are a guide only as children differ in their ability to master certain steps. With close supervision, younger children may be able to manage, although their attention span may not last until the project is finished. We have used the word <u>adult</u> **to show where help is needed, where toxic products are to be used, or where sharp instruments are to be used.**

✔ An old shirt or a garbage bag with head and arm holes cut out will make a good cover-up to keep clothing clean.

✔ Newspaper or old plastic bags will protect the work surface and make cleaning easier.

✔ Keep old rags and sponges handy for cleaning up.

✔ Shallow containers, such as ice-cream containers are useful to hold water for painting and are less likely to be tipped over than tumblers.

✔ Plastic lids, such as those from ice-cream containers make great paint palettes.

✔ Soda water helps to break up and remove dry paint stains from the carpet.

What you'll need:

Brushes: Brushes with thick handles such as shaving brushes are easy for young children to hold. Provide a brush for each paint colour; if the brush has a coloured handle, match it with the paint colour to encourage children to return the brush to the original paint pot. Over time a variety of brushes should be given to children; vary the size and type of brush and try alternatives such as feathers and household brushes.

Clay: Natural clay is excellent for modelling. It can be cut with twine or wire, and needs to be kept moist by wrapping in plastic or a wet cloth.

Collage: Artwork made from various materials glued, taped or stapled to a surface is collage. An endless variety of materials can be used for collage. Arrange separate containers of materials on a trolley or tray and provide paper, plastic, fabric, cardboard, egg cartons and boxes to use as the collage base. Make sure a glue brush is available for each child. Provide young children with small pieces of material; older children can cut their own. See collage activities for suggested collage materials. Don't overlook the possibilities of natural materials such as grass, flowers, etc..

Cornflour paste: Is made by mixing about 2 tablespoons of cornflour with enough cold water to form a paste in a saucepan. Add about 1 cup of water and cook on the stove until it reaches custard consistency. Store in the refrigerator. Add to ordinary paint for fingerpainting; add food colouring and use as fingerpaint; use as an economical extender for paint; use as a paper glue or use in papier mache.

Crayons: Pre-school-age children should be given large, thick crayons. Remove paper wrapper to encourage full use. Child care experts suggest breaking the crayons to overcome the child's apprehension of the consequences of him/her breaking them.

Dye: Readily available from department, art and craft stores. Most are more effective on natural fibres rather than synthetics.

Felt pens: Available in many colours. Ensure pens are non-toxic and give thick pens to young children.

Food colouring: Widely available in supermarkets and can be used to colour craft materials and as a substitute for Edicol; colours will be less intense. Colouring can be mixed with cornflour paste to make fingerpaint.

Glue: Any non-toxic glues can be used for children's craft. PVA glue is used often in our projects. It will hold most materials and can be thinned with water. For less permanent bonds, try flour and water pastes.

Needles: Children over 5 years old can use needles but they should be blunt and have a large eye. When weaving wool, tape can be wrapped around the end of a thread to stiffen the thread instead of using a needle.

Oil pastels: Are smooth and vividly coloured. The effect is like oily chalk.

Paint: Any non-toxic paint is suitable. Also encourage experimentation with food colouring, berry juices, glue, painting with water on the garden fence, brick wall etc.

Edicol: A non-toxic vegetable dye available in powder form. Edicol is available in half or one kilogram containers, which are expensive but will last for years. Mix Edicol with water for a clear, bright water paint, or add a cornflour paste (recipe at left) to make a thick paint.

Fabric paint: Various brands are available from art, craft and department stores. Use when permanent prints on fabric are required.

Fingerpaint: Any thick non-toxic paint can be used for fingerpainting. Fingerpaint can be made by adding Edicol or tempera paint to cornflour paste (recipe at left).

Tempera: Available in a variety of colours in powder and paint form. To mix the powder to a paint, add water and mix, then add cornflour paste .

Paint rollers: Useful as an alternative to brushes.

Paper: Newsprint is cheap, available in large sheets, absorbent and is therefore suitable for painting. Pro-vide children with a variety of paper for painting, printing and collage. Tissue, cellophane, foil, crepe and shiny coloured paper are inspirational.

Papier mache: A technique where paper pieces are dipped in paste and applied to a mould in layers, or paper pulp is used to model shapes then left to dry.

Paste: See glue.

Plaster bandage: These are gauze bandages impregnated with plaster and available from chemists. To use, just wet and place over a mould. They dry quickly and are great for mask making and sculpture.

Plasticine: Many colours are available. It can sometimes be hard for little hands to manipulate, especially in cold weather.

Printing: An impression of an object on paper or fabric is a print. Printing tools can be easily made from wood blocks and cardboard rollers, or use objects such as leaves, fruit and kitchen gadgets.

Scissors: Invest in small scissors with a blunt end. They are usually sharper than the cheap ones and are easy for little hands to use.

Staplers: Medium size staplers are easiest for children to use.

Tape: Adhesive tape in a heavy dispenser is easy to use.

EXTRAS TO COLLECT

These materials will be handy for collage, construction, painting, printing and many other children's crafts.

bark
beads and buttons
bottle tops
boxes and containers
cardboard sheets, cylinders
clock parts
confetti
corks
corrugated cardboard
cotton reels
cotton wool
egg cartons
fabric scraps
foam pieces
fur
greeting cards, postcards
hair curlers
magazines
match sticks, matchboxes
mesh
old clean socks
old telephone books
orange and onion bags
paper and card
paper clips
pasta (dry)
plastic containers
polystyrene pieces
rubber bands
sandpaper
seeds
shells
springs
squirt and spray bottles
sticks
straws
wire, wire coathangers
wood off-cuts
wool, string, thread

SAFETY FIRST

✓ Activities that involve small objects, such as polystyrene, beads and buttons should be kept for older children, over 5 years. There is a high risk that younger children will put these objects in mouths, ears or noses.

✓ Before buying or using craft materials check labels to ensure that all felt pens, crayons, play dough, paints and glues are non-toxic. Play dough can be made at home with edible dye.

✓ Supervise children using scissors to avoid cuts and wounds. Make sure all scissors are put away after use. Choose scissors with a blunt end.

✓ Supervise all use of string and cord so that children do not use it to cut off circulation or breathing.

✓ Older children only should use needles and these should be blunt-ended. Make sure all needles and pins are put away after use.

✓ Supervise all washing up of art and craft tools after use. Water is dangerous and children can drown in a small amount of water.

Tips provided by Child Safety Centre, The Children's Hospital, Camperdown, NSW.

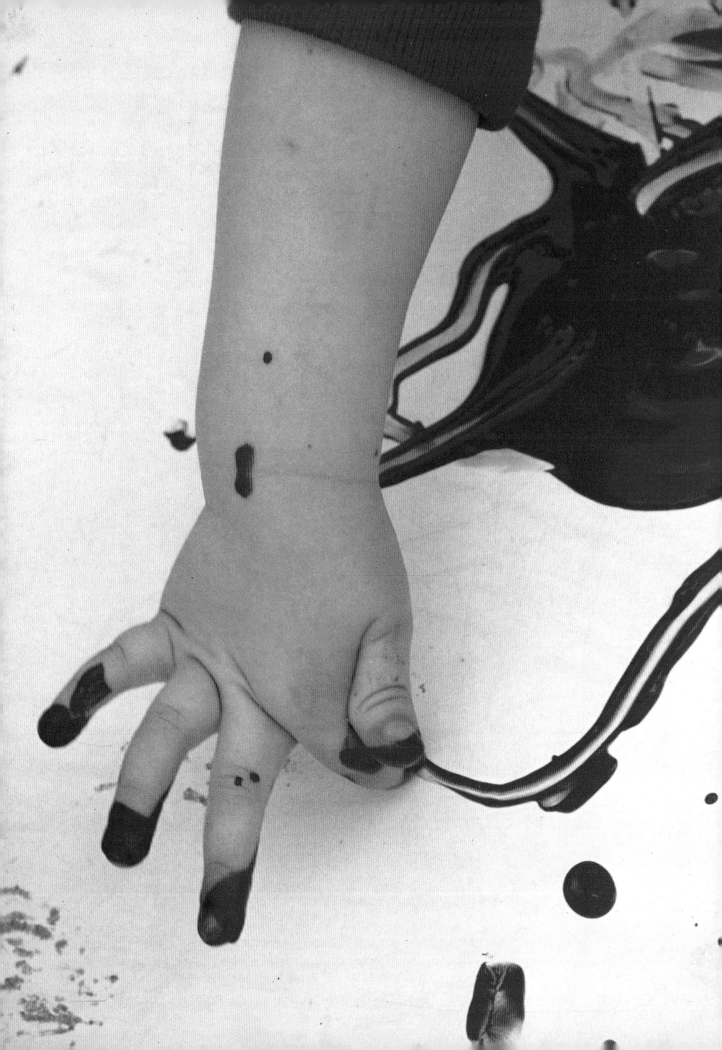

Painting

Painting opens up a world of colour and communication while providing relaxation and release of emotions. Give young children easy-to-hold painting tools, such as shaving brushes, rollers, spray bottles and foam pieces which will stimulate creativity.
Adults should avoid expecting a specific result or "picture"; just allow the child to experiment.

Fingerpainting

You will need:

Fingerpaint (see Glossary for recipe), 1-3 colours in containers with large spoon
Laminated tabletop
Grout scrapers (from hardware store)
Plastic combs
Large paper sheets (for prints)
Aprons

1. Put on aprons.

2. Spoon the paint onto the tabletop. Spread paint with hands to mix colours and enjoy the sensory experience. Make patterns and pictures with hands and fingers, moving them all over the tabletop.

Adult. Have a large dish of warm, soapy water at the ready for paint-soaked hands . Remove aprons as soon as painting is finished to avoid getting paint on clothing. Adults should also try to refrain from saying "yuk" as the child paints!

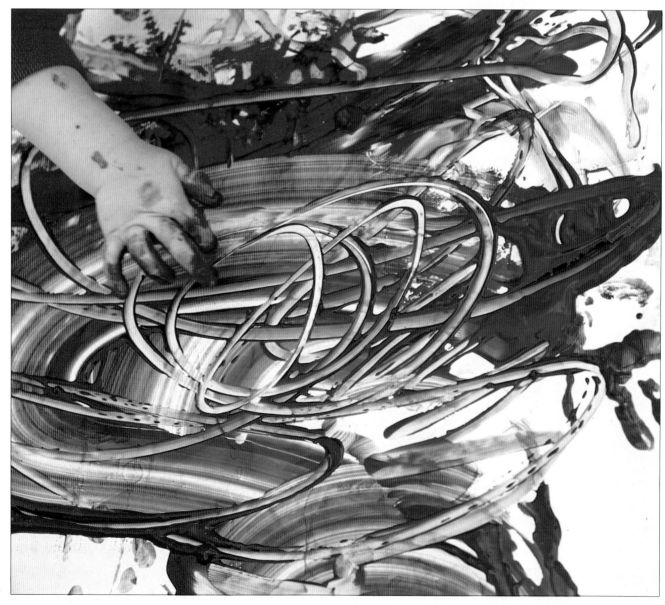

SCRAPER PAINTING

An excellent extension activity for older children is to use grout scrapers and combs to make patterns in the paint. Patterns can be made by scraping in straight lines or swirling movements.

Note. Some small fastidious children, may be reluctant to fingerpaint. They may prefer to use a roller to spread the paint and a cautious fingertip to paint patterns. Emphasise that finger-painting isn't dirty.

FINGERPAINT PRINTS

To take a print of the fingerpainting, place a large sheet of paper over the tabletop, rub over it lightly and lift it off carefully. Hang to dry. Also try taking two prints, with the same piece of paper, in different positions.

Fingerpainting is wonderful for releasing tension and anger while developing concentration and hand-eye coordination.

Spray paint mural ✏✏✏

You will need:

Thin water paint, such as Edicol, in
    red, yellow and blue
Spray bottles
Paper roll
Tape
Apron

1. Adult. Tape paper along a fence ,
a brick wall or tape pieces onto an
easel. Pour paint into spray bottles.

2. Put on apron. Squirt the paint onto
paper. Colours will mix and overlap,
creating patterns on the paper.

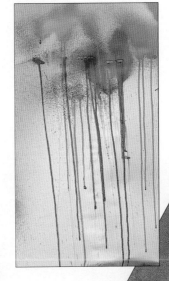

*A spray paint mural is a
colourful party activity
and makes a beautiful
decoration.*

Brush discovery painting

You will need:

Paint, Edicol water paint or tempera
  mix
Collection of brushes (e.g.shaving,
  pastry, kitchen, toothbrush, small
  house painting brushes)
Paper
Apron

1. Put on apron.

2. Use the different brushes to paint,
exploring the various effects given by
each one.

3. Colour coordinate the brushes
with the paints. This is a good colour
matching exercise for children and
keeps paints pure.

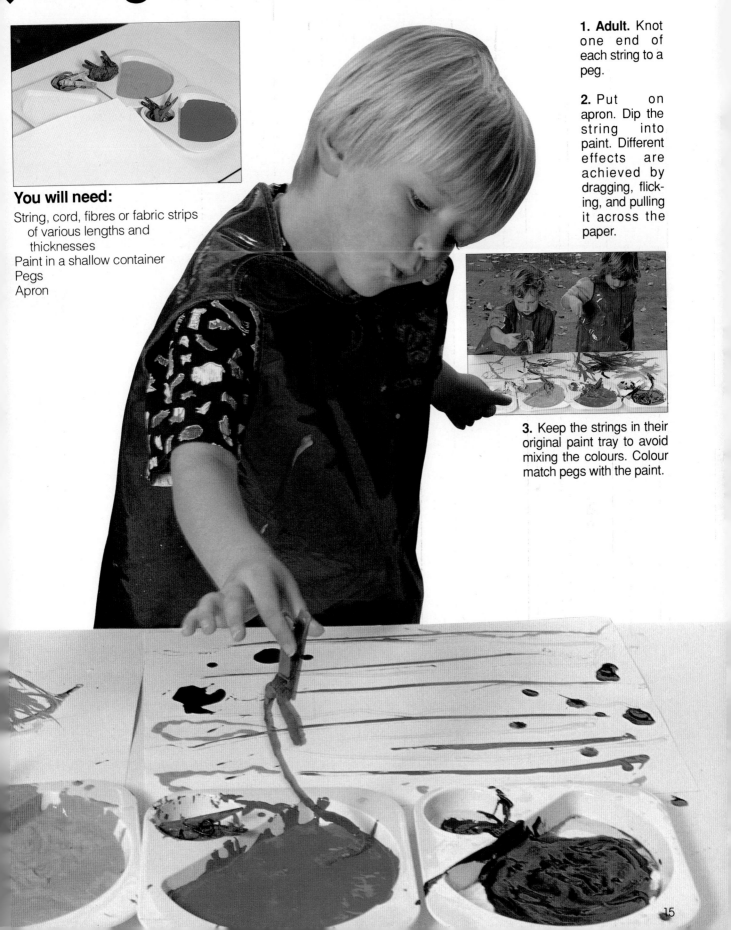

String and fibre painting

OVER 3 YEARS

You will need:

String, cord, fibres or fabric strips
　　of various lengths and
　　thicknesses
Paint in a shallow container
Pegs
Apron

1. Adult. Knot one end of each string to a peg.

2. Put on apron. Dip the string into paint. Different effects are achieved by dragging, flicking, and pulling it across the paper.

3. Keep the strings in their original paint tray to avoid mixing the colours. Colour match pegs with the paint.

Sponge painting

You will need:

Small sponge pieces
Pegs
Paint, small amount in a container
Paper
Apron

1. Put on aprons. Hold sponge pieces with a peg.

2. Dip sponge into the paint and use it to dab, or brush, making pictures and patterns.

3. Keep the sponge pieces in their original paint tray to avoid mixing colours. It also helps to colour match the peg with the paint, for example, blue peg with blue paint, etc..

 # Roller painting

OVER 3 YEARS

You will need:

Water paint, such as Edicol, in red,
  yellow and blue
Shallow containers
Foam rollers, preferably small
Paper, absorbent not shiny
Apron

1. Put on apron.

2. Spread the paint with rollers, trying different techniques, for example, waves or stripes.

3. Encourage children to replace rollers in original colour containers as paint blends quickly.

Magic painting

You will need:

Candles
Thin water paint, such as Edicol
Paper, absorbent not shiny
Brushes (shaving brushes are easy
    for small children to hold) or
    rollers
Apron

1. Put on apron. Draw on the paper using the candle.

2. Paint over the wax design using a brush and one or more colours. The wax design resists the paint and shows through clearly, just like magic!

Try using crayons instead of candles; black is most effective.

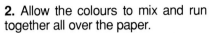 Monster painting

You will need:

Paper
Thin water paint, such as Edicol
Brushes or rollers
Felt pens
Apron

1. Put on apron. Paint over the paper with several colours .

2. Allow the colours to mix and run together all over the paper.

3. Hang painting to dry.

4. With the help of an adult, find monster faces in the painting. Outline the faces using a felt pen.

Children's imaginations will work overtime on this activity.

Printing

A print is an impression of an object on fabric or paper. Children will enjoy immediate results and a sense of accomplishment while experimenting with repetition and design. Printing tools used in our projects include tennis balls, balloons, blocks and household gadgets. The world is full of interesting shapes and patterns, look around, ordinary objects can make the most wonderful prints.

◆ Foam prints

How to make a foam print pad: Place a thin sponge in a shallow tray or bowl. Spread paint onto the sponge. To print just press the printing object onto the sponge. The sponge loads a minimum amount of paint, evenly distributed, which helps to give a clear print.

You will need:

Thick foam
Paint
Foam paint pads
Paper
Scissors
Apron

1. Adult. Spread paint onto foam paint pads. Using scissors cut thick foam into shapes. Shapes could be Christmas symbols, Easter eggs, geometric patterns, animals or letters. Older children can cut out their own printing shapes.

2. Put on apron. Press foam shape onto paint pad then onto paper to make a print. Continue printing, using different colours and shapes until you are satisfied with the effect.

3. Use a long strip of paper to create a wall frieze; large sheets to make wrapping paper; or small pieces for gift cards.

4. Hang prints to dry. Wash paint from foam printing shapes.

Mesh dab-prints

You will need:

Plastic mesh bags (onion bags)
Foam, fibre filling or fabric scraps
Paint on foam pads in trays
Paper
Apron

1. Adult. Make mesh dabbers by filling plastic mesh squares with rag, foam or fibre. (Pantihose and other fabrics could be used instead of plastic mesh bags.) Tie firmly with string. Spread paint onto foam paint pads.

2. Put on apron. Press the dabber onto the foam paint pad. Press it onto the paper. To avoid paint colours mixing, return dabbers to their original paint pad.

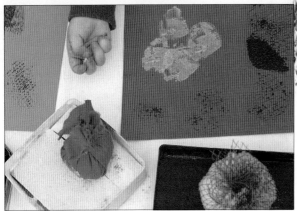

Dabbers make easy-to-hold printing tools for young children.

◆ Tennis ball prints

OVER 3 YEARS

You will need:

Tennis balls (one for each paint colour)
Thin water-based paint (Edicol or tempera)
Paper
Shallow containers for paint
Apron

1. Put on apron. Dip the tennis balls in paint.

2. Dab or drop the balls on paper to make a print.

3. Keep the balls in their original paint container to avoid mixing colours.

4. Hang or lay prints flat to dry. If prints are hung, the paint tends to run and add interest to the patterns created. If you want clear splatter prints leave the prints to dry flat.

Use Christmas colours to print festive wrapping paper.

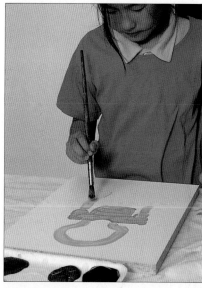 Mono-printed doll

OVER 6 YEARS

You will need:

Printing surface such as a
  laminated board, ceramic tile,
  heavy plastic, thick glass
Fabric paint
Cotton fabric
Polyester fibre filling
Raffia or wool for hair
Ribbon
Felt scraps
Needle and sewing thread or
  sewing machine
Apron

1. Put on apron. Paint the front of the doll on the printing surface.

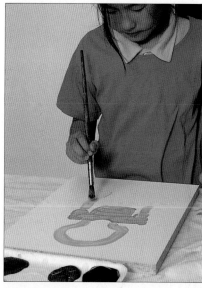

2. Place a fabric piece over the design and press gently with an open hand, without rubbing.

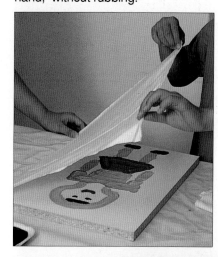

3. Lift the fabric carefully, without moving it sideways. Hang the print to dry. Clean and dry the printing surface and paint a back view of the doll. Make a second print and leave to dry. Iron both fabric pieces to fix the paint.

4. Place both fabric pieces together and cut out around the doll, leaving a 2cm allowance. Avoid having very narrow sections of fabric as these will be difficult to fill with fibre.

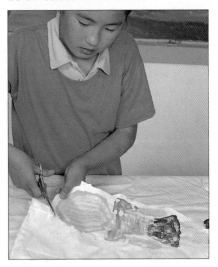

5. Adult. Pin the two fabric pieces together with the printed sides to the inside. Stitch around the shape with a needle and thread, or sewing machine, and using a 2cm-wide seam. Leave a 10cm opening in the stitching (for the fibre filling).

6. Turn through to right side and stuff with fibre filling. Carefully stitch the 10cm opening closed.

7. Take a length of raffia or wool strands and plait each end, leaving an unplaited section in the centre. Glue the unplaited section onto the doll's head to make hair, leaving the plaits free. Tie plaits with ribbon. Add buttons, eyes or felt nose as desired.

A reverse-print variation can be made by brushing paint over the printing surface and scraping a design into the paint.

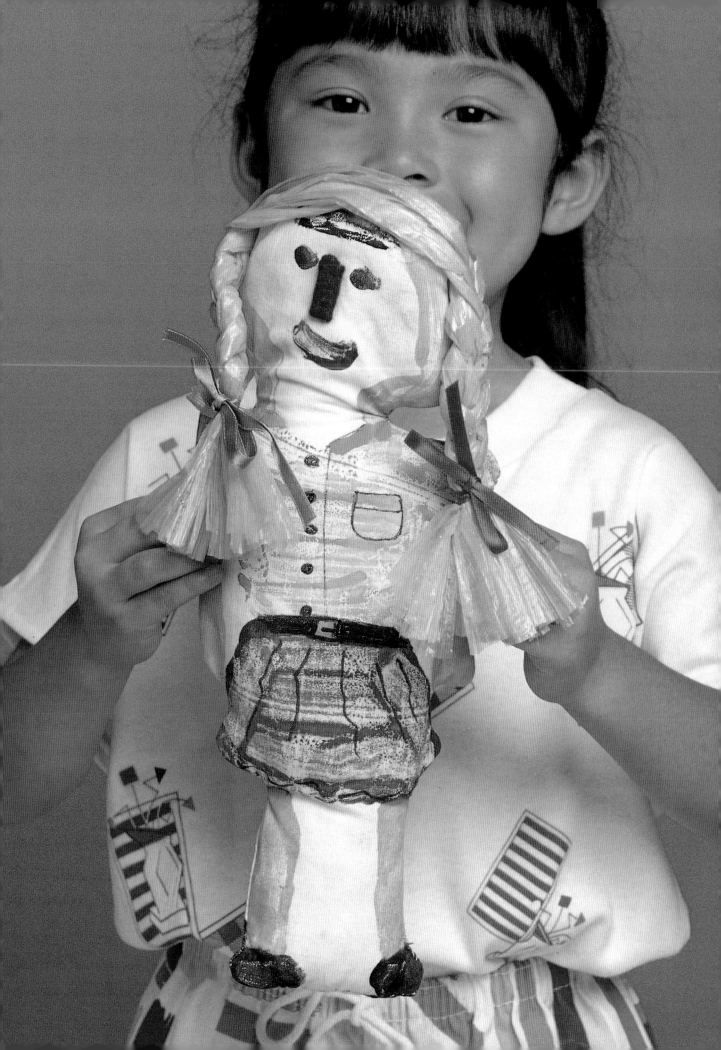

Spool printing

You will need:

Spools of various sizes and shapes
Paint
Foam paint pad
Paper
Apron

1. Adult. Spread paint onto foam paint pad.

2. Put on apron. Press the spool onto paint pad. Press the spool onto paper.

3. Continue printing using different spools and colours.

Glue prints onto cardboard and cover with adhesive plastic to make bright placemats.

Block print stamp

OVER 3 YEARS

You will need:

Wood block (offcut)
Thick string or wool
Fabric or garment (for printing)
Fabric paint
Paint roller
PVA glue
Brush (optional)
Apron

1. Put on apron. Brush or squirt glue onto the wood block in an interesting pattern.

2. Arrange string or wool pieces on the glue. Avoid overlapping any pieces of string or wool. Leave to dry.

3. Roll or brush paint onto the string-covered side of the block.

This method is great for printing large sheets of paper for gift wrap.

4. Spread out the garment or fabric so it is completely flat. If printing a garment, put sheets of paper between the front and back of the garment to avoid paint soaking through both fabric layers. Carefully place the wood block, string-side down, onto the fabric. Press gently then lift the block off the fabric without moving it sideways. Repeat the print over the fabric as desired.

⬦ Balloon prints

OVER 3 YEARS

You will need:

Partly inflated balloons
Paint
Paper
Apron

1. Adult. Place one balloon in each container of paint.

2. Put on apron. Dab the paint-covered balloon onto the paper. The knotted end makes a useful handle.

3. Continue printing using different paint colours. Return balloons to their original paint container after use to avoid mixing colours.

4. Hang prints to dry.

Roller printing

You will need:

Foam pieces, wool, string or tyre
    inner tube
Cardboard cylinder
Thick paint
Large sheet of paper
Foam print pad
PVA glue
Apron

1. Put on apron. Glue pieces of foam shapes, wool, string or tyre inner tube around the cardboard cylinder.

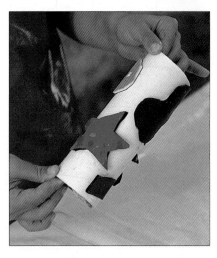

2. Load one sponge with paint and rest it on the other two sponges or load foam pad with paint. Roll the cylinder on the paint pad then roll it over the paper. Repeat the print until the paper is covered.

*Try materials of different
textures to vary the print.*

Kitchen gadget printing

You will need:

Kitchen gadgets such as ice block
    trays, strainers, whisks,
    containers, biscuit cutters, and
    any gadget with an interesting
    shape which has a flat surface
Foam paint pads
Paint
Large sheets of paper
Apron

1. Adult. Spread paint onto foam
paint pad.

2. Put on apron. Press printing
gadget onto paint pad.

3. Stamp gadget onto paper to make
a print. Continue printing with different
objects until the print is complete.

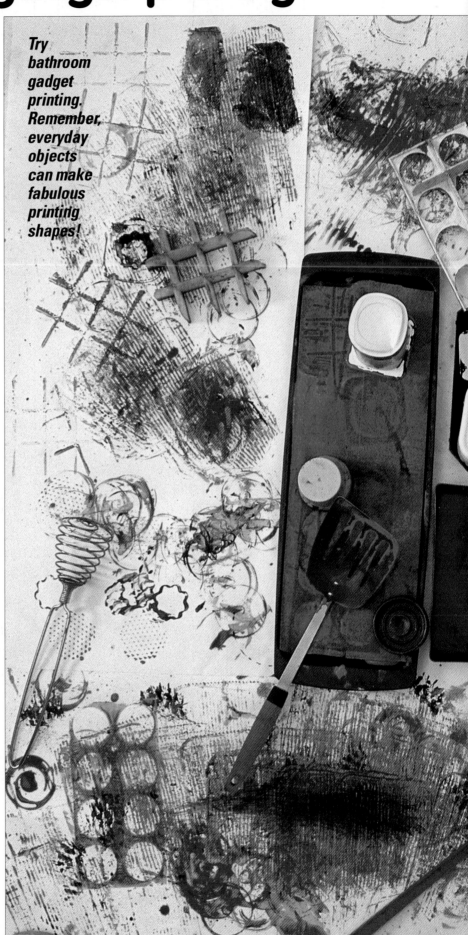

*Try
bathroom
gadget
printing.
Remember,
everyday
objects
can make
fabulous
printing
shapes!*

Crayon screen printing

You will need:

Silk screen
Squeegee
Fabric paint
Fabric or garment (for printing)
Oil pastels
Mineral turpentine
Cleaning rag
Apron

1. Put on apron. Using oil pastels draw a picture or pattern directly onto the mesh of the screen.

2. Draw over the design again until the oil pastel lines are quite thick.

3. If printing a garment place paper between the front and back to avoid paint soaking through both layers of fabric. Place the screen onto the fabric or garment. Spoon a thick strip of paint along one side of the screen. More than one colour can be used.

4. Have an adult or friend hold the screen firmly. Drag the squeegee across the surface of the screen, spreading the paint evenly. Repeat this two or three times; more than one colour can be used.

5. Carefully lift the screen, raising it from one side to the other. Remove excess paint from the screen.

6. Adult. Saturate a rag with turpentine and scrub the oil pastel pattern off the screen. Wash the screen thoroughly with cool water.

7. Hang the fabric or garment to dry. Before wearing or washing, iron the fabric to fix the paint.

For a different effect, screen print a picture onto coloured paper or cardboard .

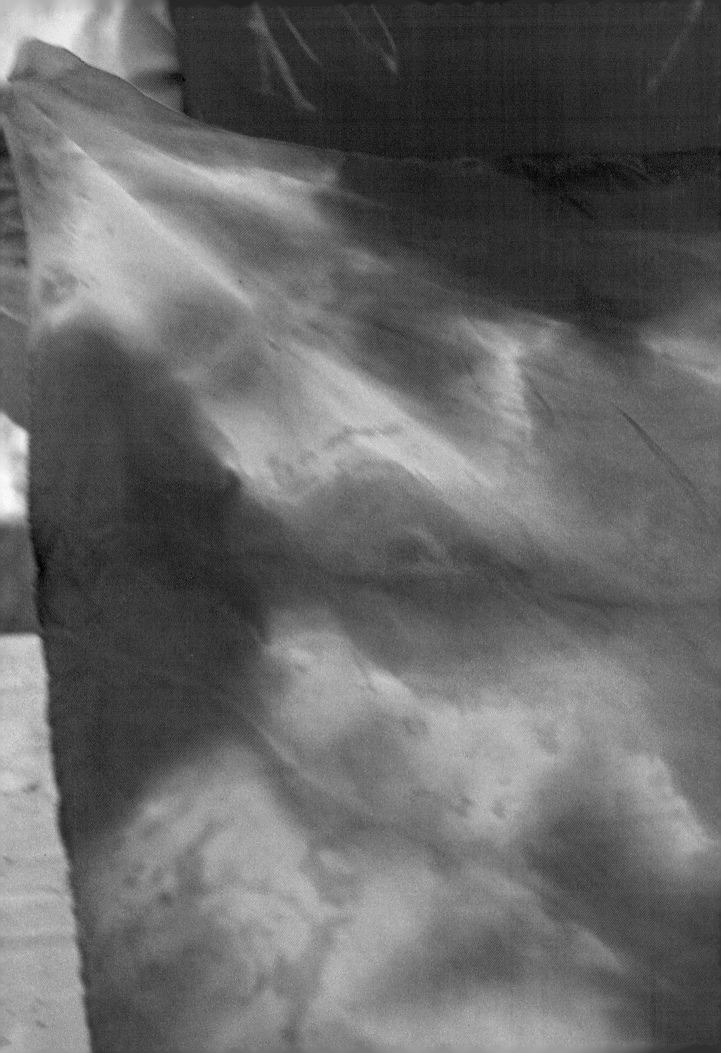

Dyeing

Dyeing is an easy way of colouring fabric. Results are quick, often spectacular, and give a sense of satisfaction and accomplishment – a boost to any child's self esteem. Use of multiple colours helps children learn about colour mixing while dyed fabric has many uses.

Dip and dye

You will need:

Edicol dyes or cold water fabric
  dyes, several colours
White cotton fabric
Rubber gloves
Containers for dye

1. Adult. Mix dyes in separate containers according to the manufacturer's directions.

2. Fold the fabric several times to make a small triangle or square.

3. Put on rubber gloves. Dip each corner of the folded fabric into a different coloured dye. Allow the dyes to meet in the centre of the fabric. Squeeze out excess dye after each dye application.

4. Open out the fabric. Hang to dry.

Dyed fabric makes a terrific cushion cover, tablecloth or a striking wall hanging.

40

◆ Multi-coloured tie-dyeing

You will need:

Two or three primary-colour dyes
   (red, yellow or blue)
Dye fix (if necessary)
White cotton garment or fabric
Rubber bands or string
Rubber gloves
Containers for dye

1. Adult. Mix dyes in separate containers according to the manufacturer's directions.

2. Bunch or roll the fabric and bind it tightly at intervals with rubber bands or string wrapping over the same spot several times.

3. Put on rubber gloves and submerge the fabric in one dye bucket for a few minutes. Remove and leave it until it is semi-dry then remove string and bands. Allow to dry thoroughly.

4. Bunch or roll the fabric in a different direction and tie again tightly.

5. Submerge tied fabric in the second dye colour. Remove, leave to dry. Dip in a third dye, if desired.

6. Remove bands or string to see the effect. Hang to dry.

Reverse tie-dyeing

You will need:

Liquid bleach
Cotton garment or fabric in dark
 colour (black, dark blue and blue
 denim work well)
String or rubber bands
Rubber gloves
Container for bleach

1. Adult. Pour bleach into a stable container.

2. Fold, twist, crumple or roll the fabric then tie tightly with string or rubber bands.

3. Put on rubber gloves and dip the fabric in bleach until the colour of the fabric changes.

4. Rinse thoroughly in cold water then remove the bands or string. Hang to dry.

Be careful using bleach.
Avoid contact with skin!

Peg dyeing

You will need:

Edicol dye or cold water fabric dye
White cotton fabric
Clothes pegs or bulldog clips
Rubber gloves
Container for dye

1. Adult. Mix dye according to the manufacturer's directions.

2. Fold fabric as desired, until quite small. Place pegs or bulldog clips around the fabric. The pegs or clips will form a barrier to the dye, creating a pattern.

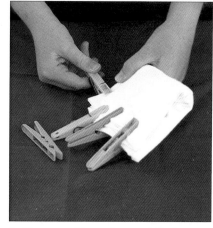

3. Put on rubber gloves. Briefly submerge the fabric in the dye. Remove the pegs or clips and open the fabric. Hang to dry.

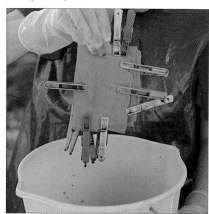

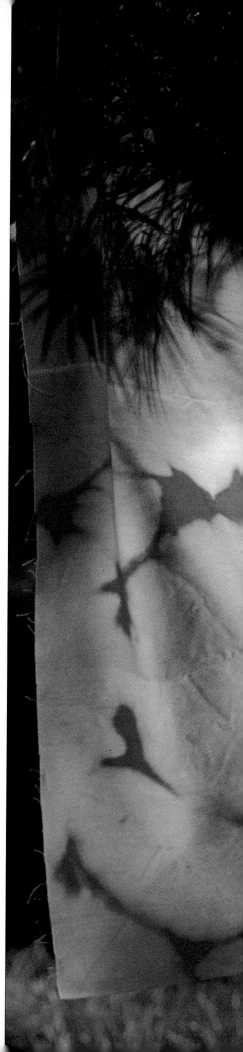

44

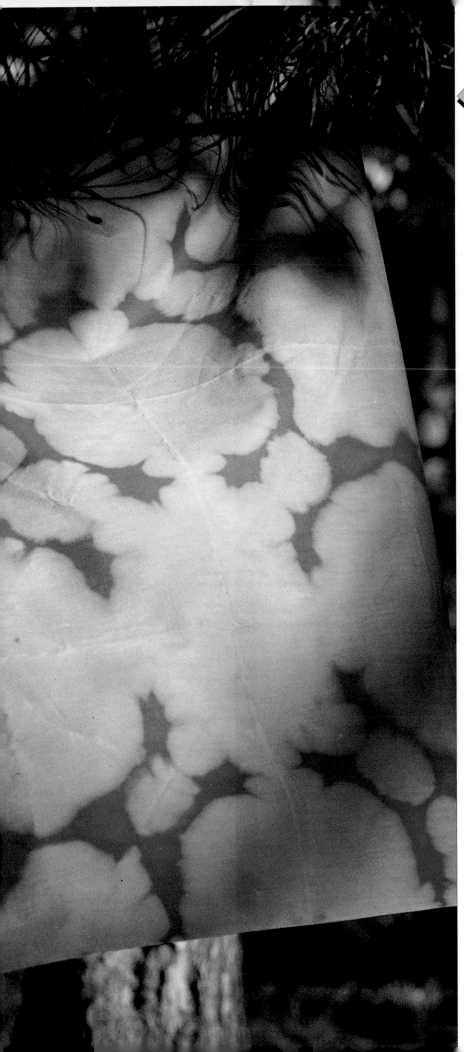

Reverse dip and dye

OVER 6 YEARS

You will need:

Liquid bleach
Dark-coloured cotton fabric (black, dark blue and blue denim work well)
Rubber gloves
Container for bleach

1. Adult. Pour bleach into a stable container.

2. Fold the fabric into a triangle or square until it is quite small.

3. Put on rubber gloves then dip each corner of the folded fabric piece into bleach. Hold each corner in the bleach until it changes colour.

4. Open out fabric. Hang to dry

Be careful using bleach. Avoid contact with skin!

Touch
and
Feel

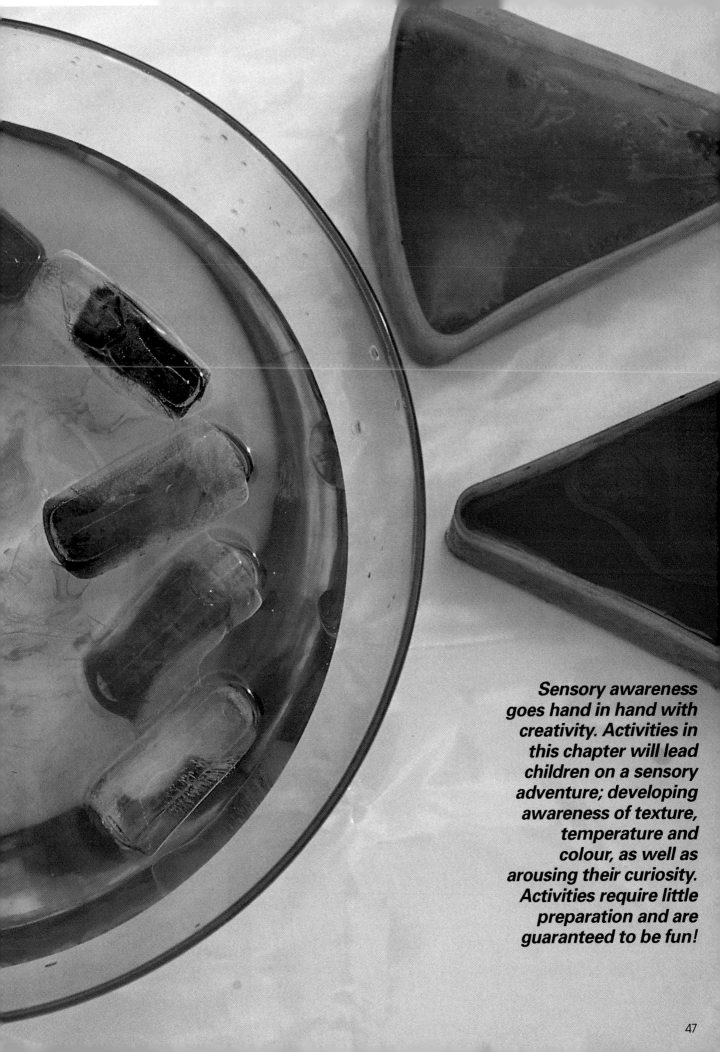

Sensory awareness goes hand in hand with creativity. Activities in this chapter will lead children on a sensory adventure; developing awareness of texture, temperature and colour, as well as arousing their curiosity. Activities require little preparation and are guaranteed to be fun!

Coloured ice melts

You will need:

Food colouring
Water
Plastic containers of various sizes
  and shapes, for freezing
Large plastic containers

1. Adult with children. Add food colouring to water. Freeze the different colours of water in various containers overnight.

2. Look at the patterns formed in the ice by the food colouring; colour will either freeze evenly or coagulate in patches in the ice.

Lots of fun outdoors on a hot day!

3. Empty the coloured ice into a large container of water or into an empty container. Watch it melt; colours will mix, swirl and blend together. Dark colours are best added to the bowl last as they will eventually give a murky colour to the water.

4. Feel and watch the shapes of the melting ice and observe the mixing colours. Discuss why it melts. Children also like to touch the ice and watch whether it floats or sinks.

◆4◆ Texture rubbing

You will need:

Textured objects such as fans, bark, packaging plastic, combs, braid, laces, fabric
Crayons
Paper

1. Adult. Flimsy materials such as braid and lace can be glued or pinned onto a board to keep them rigid.

2. Select a few textured objects. Place paper over the textured surface. Rub the paper with a crayon.

3. Try mixing crayon colours and using several textured surfaces with the one piece of paper.

Variation: Make a texture rubbing as above but use white candles instead of crayons. Then paint over the paper with a thin water-based paint such as Edicol.

Slime

OVER **3** YEARS

You will need:

1 cup Lux soap flakes
2 litres warm water
Egg beaters
Kitchen gadgets such as a funnel, cup, whisk, soup ladle, scoop, soap drainers, punnets, sponges, jug, etc.
Large plastic container
A pinch of Edicol for colouring (optional)

1. Adult. Dissolve soap flakes in warm water in a large plastic container. Add Edicol, if desired. Allow mixture to stand until it becomes thick, add more water if necessary. Beat mixture with egg beaters. Children can help too!

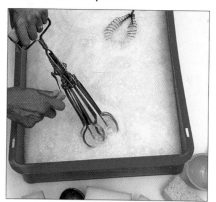

2. Use the kitchen gadgets to pour, measure, scoop, beat and whisk. Children can also use words to describe how the mixture feels and what they are doing.

Note. Younger children also enjoy slime but need careful supervision to avoid soap getting in their eyes.

Sponges are wonderful in "slime", making mounds of bubbly froth and providing great exercise for small hands.

Mix and mess

You will need:

Large containers of seeds, dried peas, beans, lentils, rice, grains, tea, cereal, etc.
Spoons, scoops, tongs, cup measures
Plastic containers for mixing

1. Adult. Arrange containers of seeds, etc. in the centre of a table outdoors or in an easy- to -clean area. Give a medium-sized container to each child for mixing.

2. Use scoops, spoons, tongs and cups to mix, measure, stir and pour, but don't eat!

Children will enjoy the texture and consistency of the ingredients and the fun of "cooking".

Floating & sinking

You will need:

Objects which will float or sink, for example, ping pong balls, golf balls, blocks, kitchen gadgets, sponges, strainers, straws, stones, flowers, corks, confetti, containers of various sizes
Large container filled with water
Food colouring (optional)

1. Adult. Working outdoors, fill the container with water. Add food colouring to the water, if desired.

2. Adult supervision. Drop the objects into the water and observe floating and sinking. Guess which objects will sink and which will float. Talk about why this happens. Children will also enjoy pouring, and squeezing water from sponges and playing with the objects in the water.

Children can close their eyes and guess which objects they touch in the water.

Goop

You will need:

2 packets of cornflour
2 cups of water
Food colouring
Plastic or newspaper-covered table,
   preferably outdoors
Large container
Aprons

1. Adult. Mix the water and colouring into the cornflour. The goop should have a thick consistency; add extra water if necessary.

2. Put on aprons. Plunge hands into the goop and feel the consistency. Use words to describe the feeling: "sticky, slimy, cool" etc..

3. Enjoy exploring the behaviour of goop; it runs through the fingers, swirls slowly and has a pleasant, heavy feeling. Patterns can be made in the air and on the table.

This activity looks messy but clean-up is quite easy; goop can be picked up or wiped off the table and easily washed off hands. However, aprons should be worn.

Construction and Collage

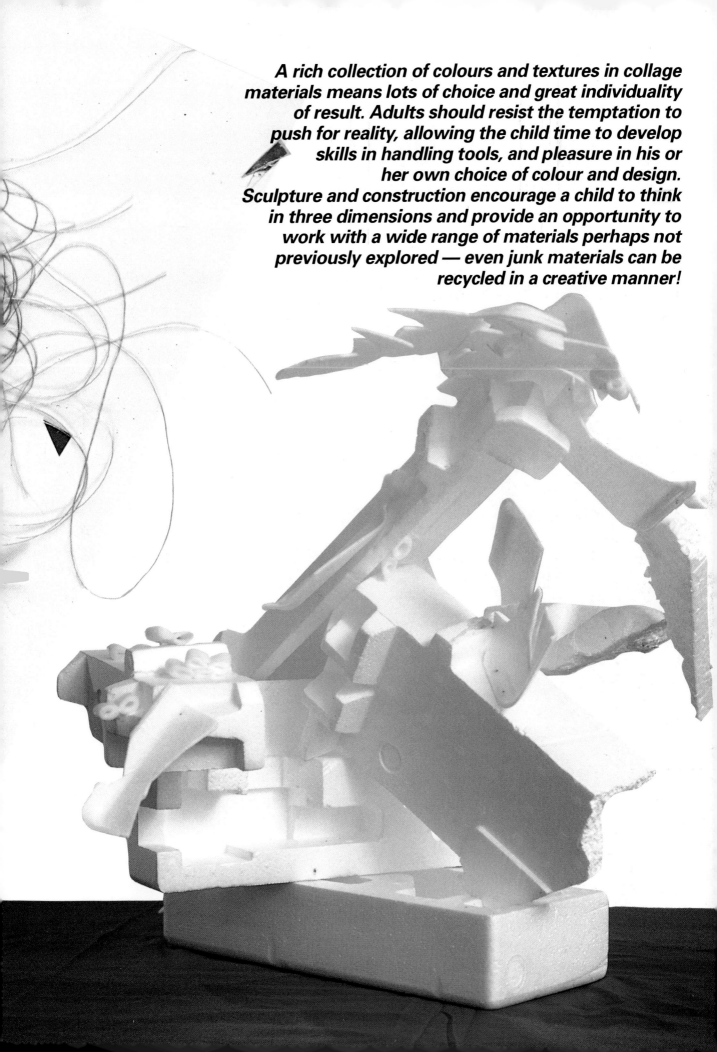

A rich collection of colours and textures in collage materials means lots of choice and great individuality of result. Adults should resist the temptation to push for reality, allowing the child time to develop skills in handling tools, and pleasure in his or her own choice of colour and design. Sculpture and construction encourage a child to think in three dimensions and provide an opportunity to work with a wide range of materials perhaps not previously explored — even junk materials can be recycled in a creative manner!

Mixed material collage

You will need:

Paper
Plastic container lids (clean)
Cardboard sheets
Cardboard boxes or cylinders
Cellophane
Tissue paper
Coloured paper
Coloured foil paper
String, yarn
Fibres, thread, cotton wool
Matchsticks
Tinsel
Plastic
Confetti
Fabric scraps
Glue (PVA will hold most materials)
Scissors
Any other suitable materials

1. Adult. Cut or tear cellophane, tissue and coloured paper into pieces. Arrange all materials in separate containers within easy reach of children, and have glue in pots with a brush for each child. Containers of collage materials can be stored and moved easily on a trolley.

2. Brush glue onto the collage base; a paper sheet, cardboard box, cylinder or plastic lid. Older children can brush glue onto the material to be glued, rather than the base.

3. Glue collage materials onto the collage base. Children can make collage pictures or three dimensional constructions using cardboard boxes and containers.

Display collages on a noticeboard or suspend three dimensional constructions from a ceiling.

OVER 6 YEARS

Polystyrene sculpture

You will need:

Polystyrene pieces
Toothpicks or pins
Stanley knife (optional)
PVA glue (optional)
Scissors

1. Plan the sculpture you will make using the polystyrene pieces. Use a large polystyrene piece as the base for the sculpture.

2. Adult supervision. Cut polystyrene pieces into shapes desired. Large pieces can be cut using a knife, thin pieces with scissors.

3. Construct the sculpture. Press pins or toothpicks through the polystyrene pieces to hold them together. Glue can be used to strengthen the joins between pieces.

Wire sculpture

OVER 8 YEARS

You will need:

Wire
Wire cutters
2cm-wide fabric strips (we used
  cotton lawn)
Plasticine block
PVA glue mix (half water, half glue)
Container for glue

1. Shape the wire into the form of an animal, a person or an interesting shape. The wire sculpture should be able to stand or recline on the plasticine block. Trim the wire ends with wire cutters.

2. Work on a plastic or newspaper covered tabletop. Dip a fabric strip in the glue mix and wrap it around the wire. Continue wrapping until wire is covered as desired.

3. Stand the figure in a plasticine block for display.

4. Leave to dry.

Try textured fabrics for wrapping or paint the fabric after the glue has dried.

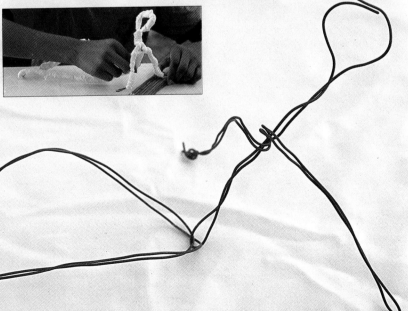

◆ Coloured glasses

You will need:

Cardboard cylinder, cone, foil meal
   tray or egg carton
Cellophane pieces
PVA glue and brush, or sticky tape
Ice cream stick (for opera glasses)
Scissors

MULTI-COLOURED GLASSES

1. To make the multi-coloured looking glasses, use an egg carton. **Adult.** Make a large hole in each cup section.

2. Glue or tape pieces of coloured cellophane over each hole. Look through the cellophane to see a colourful world.

OPERA GLASSES

1. To make opera glasses, trim around a foil meal tray. **Adult.** Cut two holes for the lenses.

2. Tape cellophane over each hole. Tape an ice cream stick in the centre or at the side of the glasses.

BINOCULARS

1. To make binoculars, tape pieces of cellophane over the end of two short cylinders. Different colours can be used for each one.

2. Tape the two cylinders together. A string can be attached, if desired.

TELESCOPE

1. To make a telescope, use a long cylinder or cone. Tape a piece of cellophane over one end of the cylinder.

You will need:

Paper or plastic sheets or lids
Coloured paper or tissue paper
Glue in tubs
Brushes
Scissors

1. Adult. Tear coloured paper or tissue paper into pieces.

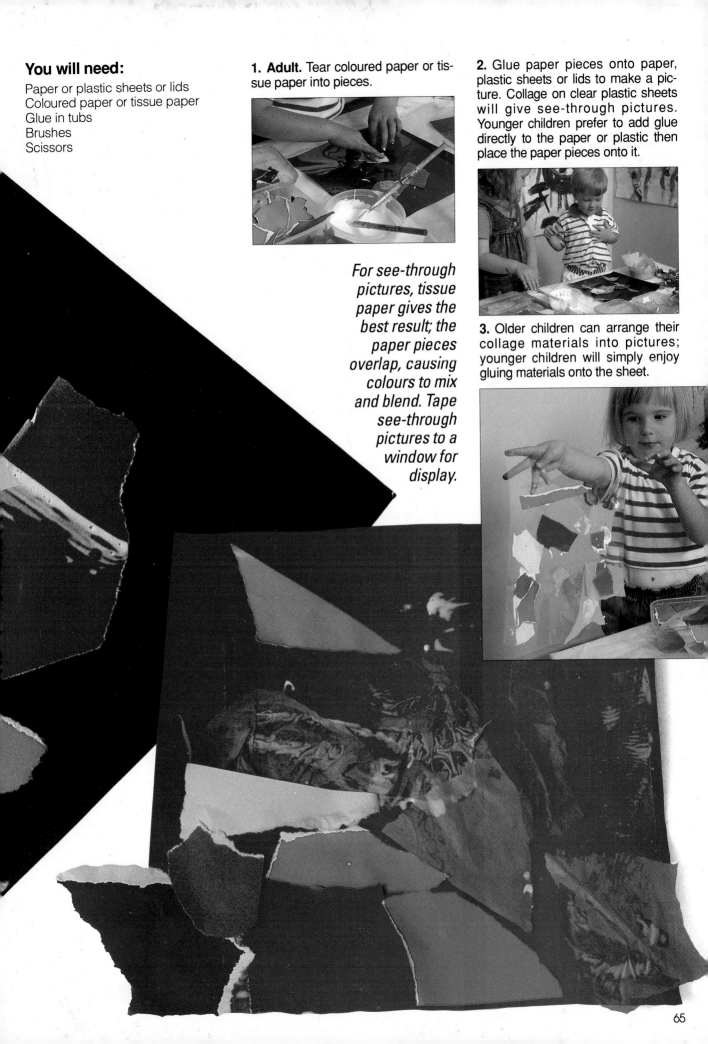

2. Glue paper pieces onto paper, plastic sheets or lids to make a picture. Collage on clear plastic sheets will give see-through pictures. Younger children prefer to add glue directly to the paper or plastic then place the paper pieces onto it.

For see-through pictures, tissue paper gives the best result; the paper pieces overlap, causing colours to mix and blend. Tape see-through pictures to a window for display.

3. Older children can arrange their collage materials into pictures; younger children will simply enjoy gluing materials onto the sheet.

Masks and Hats

Masks allow a child to be magically transformed into another person or creature. Behind the mask the wearer can do almost anything from the bravest deed to the funniest trick, without inhibition.
Also included in this chapter are hats which are simple to make and fun to wear.

 # New faces

You will need:

Face pictures, cut from magazines
Light cardboard
Ice cream sticks
Masking tape
Glue
Scissors

1. Glue pictures onto cardboard. Carefully trim around the picture. Use eyes, nose and mouth to make separate masks or use the whole face. Small lookout holes can be cut out for eyes. Older children can find and cut out their own pictures.

2. Tape a stick onto the back of each picture, at the side or bottom.

3. Use as a mask to make a new face. It's suprising what a difference they make.

Attach your new face to elastic to wear at masquerade parties. Older children and even adults will be in gales of laughter!

◆ Cone hats

You will need:

Lightweight coloured cardboard
Ribbons and sequins
Glitter
Flowers and other decorations
Adhesive tape or staples
Glue
Scissors
Elastic (optional)

1. Adult. Cut a circle of cardboard; the size of the circle will determine the height of the hat. Older children can cut their own cardboard circle.

2. Cut a slit from one edge into the centre of the cardboard circle. Overlap the two edges of the slit until the cone shape fits the head. Hold the cone hat together with adhesive tape or staples.

3. Glue or staple ribbons, sequins, glitter and other decorations to the hat as desired.

4. Adult. Make a hole through each side of the hat. Cut a length of elastic, long enough to pass under the child's chin, and tie through the holes.

 Papier mache mask with clay mould

(over 8 years symbol)

You will need:

Block of clay
Thin plastic wrap
Newspaper or telephone book
    pages
Glue mix (½ PVA glue + ½ water)
Container for glue mix
Paint
Brush
Fabric strips or fringing (for hair)
Cord

1. Working on a plastic or newspaper covered tabletop, mould the clay to form the face of a person, fantasy creature or animal.

71

2. Cover the clay mould with plastic wrap, making sure it clings closely to the clay.

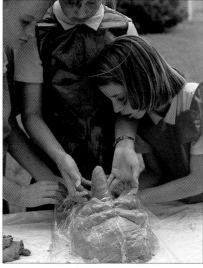

3. Tear paper into small pieces. Dip newspaper pieces into the glue mix and place on the plastic-wrapped clay mould. Continue adding glue-dipped newspaper until you have built up four or five layers. If using telephone book pages apply a layer of white paper followed by a layer of yellow paper to ensure an even layer is applied. Leave to dry overnight.

4. Remove the mask from the clay mould then paint and decorate as desired. We glued on fabric strips for hair. For hanging, punch holes at each side and attach a cord across the back of the mask.

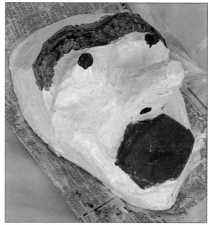

Pictures of tribal or carnival masks will provide lots of inspiration!

◆ Party hats

OVER 2 YEARS

You will need:

Paper plates
Tissue paper pieces
Strips of cellophane
Coloured threads
Tinsel
Cake papers
String
Glue and brushes
Scissors

*Make and wear hats
at a party before the
food is served!*

1. Brush glue onto bottom of the paper plate.

2. Apply tissue paper strips, threads, cellophane, and other decorations to the hat.

3. Adult. Punch holes and attach string ties on each side of the hat to hold it in place when being worn.

Plaster bandage mask

You will need:

Plaster bandage (from a pharmacy)
Vaseline
Container of water
Paint
Brush
Ribbon or cord
Scissors

1. This activity should be carefully supervised by an **adult**. Cut the plaster bandage into strips approximately 4cm-long.

2. Adult supervision. Tie back the child's hair and generously coat the face with vaseline.

3. Dip a piece of bandage in the water and place it on the child's face.

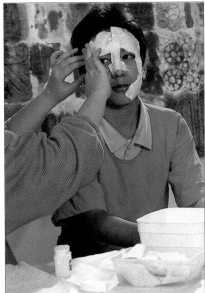

Use the mask as a wall decoration when it's not being worn.

4. Adult supervision. Avoiding the nostrils, mouth and eyes, continue the plastering process, overlapping each bandage piece until the entire face is well covered.

Note. Be careful not to cover the nostrils, mouth or eyes.

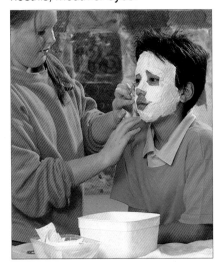

5. Strengthen the mask by adding another layer of plaster bandage. To remove the mask, gently lift the edges to break the suction, then carefully lift the mask from the face.

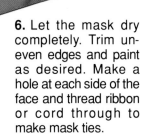

6. Let the mask dry completely. Trim uneven edges and paint as desired. Make a hole at each side of the face and thread ribbon or cord through to make mask ties.

Chicken wire mask

You will need:

Chicken wire
Wire cutters
Newspaper or telephone book
Glue mix (½ PVA + ½ water)
PVA glue
Fringing or curled paper for hair
Paint
Brush
Masking or cloth tape
Foam (optional)
Scissors

1. Adult. Cut and shape the chicken wire into a large head shape that can easily slip over the child's head and rest on their shoulders. Cover wire ends with tape for safety.

Create and use masks for a school play or write a play around the characters you make.

2. Tear newspaper or telephone book pages into large pieces. Dip large pieces of newspaper into the glue mix and then place these onto the chicken wire until it is completely covered with the paper.

3. Roll and crumple newspaper to form nose, mouth, forehead ridge, eyebrows and eyeballs. Glue features in place. We cut out ear shapes from thin cardboard.

4. Continue applying glue-dipped newspaper over features and face until you have built up about 4 layers. Allow to dry overnight.

5. Paint the mask as desired. Glue fringing or curled paper onto the head for hair.

6. Place cloth tape over the ends of the wire from the inside. If necessary, pad the inside of the mask with foam for comfort.

7. Adult. Cut one or two lookout-holes for the wearer. These may not necessarily be in the same position as eyes of the puppet.

Weaving and Stitching

Fibres, yarns and fabrics provide new tactile experiences and exercise the fine motor skills of small hands. Try not to expect each child's work to appear exactly as the pictures in this book. Treat our projects as a starting point and encourage children to develop their own ideas.

Nature weaving

OVER 5 YEARS

You will need:

4 sticks about 20cm long
String
Twigs, long grasses, fleece, weeds,
    feathers, flowers, and other
    natural materials
Scissors

1. Make a square frame by lashing the 4 sticks together with string at each corner.

2. Wind string firmly around the frame, securing each length to the stick by knotting or wrapping. Continue winding string from end to end at regular intervals until the frame is full. Tie the string ends to the frame.

3. Starting from one end, weave twigs, grasses, feathers and other materials under and over the strings. Continue until strings are covered. Hang the weaving in the frame; it makes a beautiful wall hanging.

This weaving gives children an opportunity to explore the characteristics of natural materials.

Hessian weaving

You will need:

Hessian fabric pieces
Yarn, raffia, feathers
Scissors

1. Remove threads from around the hessian fabric piece to form a fringed border on all sides.

Use the woven hessian pieces as table mats.

2. Draw out threads from the hessian in rows as desired. Withdraw threads in a block by carefully snipping then removing them.

3. Weave yarn, raffia or feathers through the spaces left by the withdrawn threads. Short lengths of raffia or yarn can be used to tie bundles of threads together.

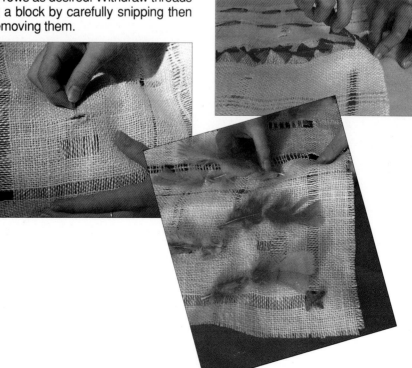

Weaving on a box loom

You will need:

Cardboard box
Ice cream sticks
Fabric strips or wool
Masking tape
Scissors

1. Tape ice-cream sticks at regular intervals along one end of the box. Tape sticks in line with the first row, at the opposite end of the box.

2. Tie a fabric strip or length of wool to the first stick at one end. Take the strip around the first stick at the other end, then up again to the next stick, pulling the fabric strip taut. Continue until all sticks are looped.

3. Beginning at one end of the box, weave fabric strips or wool under and over the first (warp) strips. Continue weaving until all the warp strips are covered.

4. When weaving is complete, slip the weaving off the sticks and thread dowel rods through the loops at each end. Secure loose ends by threading these back into the weaving.

5. Attach a hanging cord to the top dowel. Use as a wall hanging.

Make several box weavings, then join them together to make a floor mat!

Weaving on wire

OVER **6** YEARS

You will need:

Chicken wire or wire mesh
Fabric strips and yarns
Buttons or beads
Pipe cleaners (optional)
Wire cutters
Masking tape
Scissors

1. Adult. Cut the wire into the shape and size desired. It can be bent into three dimensional form or left as a flat surface. Bind the edges with masking tape to cover sharp ends.

2. Tie or weave fabric strips and yarn over and under the wire. Fabric strips can be woven in a circular pattern or back and forth across the wire. Weave over one or more wire loops to vary the weaving.

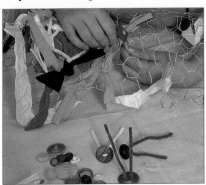

3. Twist pipe cleaners into the weaving. Thread buttons or beads onto loose ends of fabric strips or onto pipe cleaners. Add loops or knots to make the texture interesting.

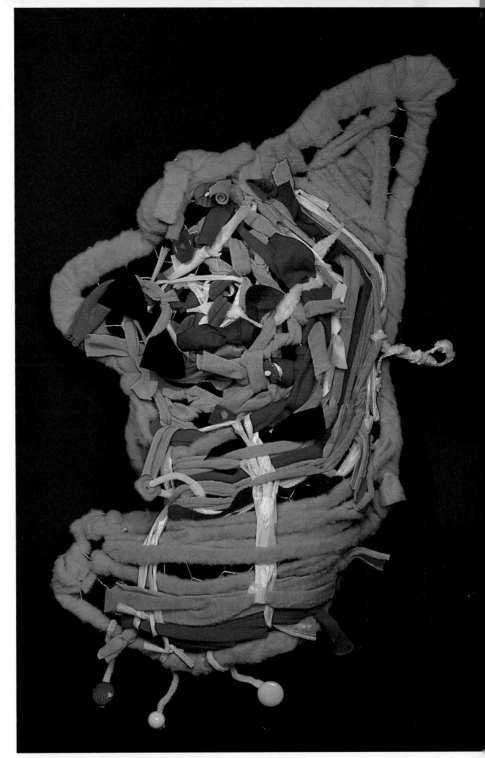

Variation: Draw a picture on paper and transfer it to the wire using crayons. The crayon will stick to the wire. Use fabric and yarns to weave the design you desire.

Drinking straw weaving

You will need:

6 drinking straws
6 one-metre-long yarns (or length
  desired)
Yarns, various colours
Scissors

1. Tie the metre-long yarns together at one end. Thread the untied ends of each yarn through a straw, push straws close to the knot.

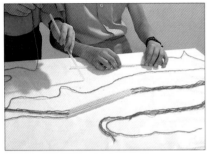

2. Tie a loose knot at the other end of the straws to hold them in place.

3. Weave coloured yarn over and under the straws. Join new yarns by tying to the previous length. When you have woven about half the length of the straws, undo the knot at the bottom and slide the straws down a little, keeping the top of the straws inside the weaving at all times.

Continue weaving until the fabric is the desired length.

4. When the weaving is finished, remove the straws and tie adjacent strings together. Trim then thread the string ends back into the weaving. Use the weaving as an unusual guitar strap or belt.

Substitute cardboard fabric rolls for straws and fabric strips for weaving yarns. This would make a larger weaving which could be used as a mat.

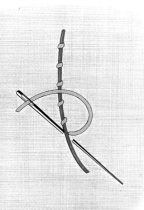

COUCHING

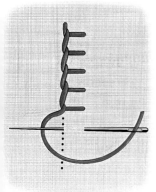

BLANKET STITCH

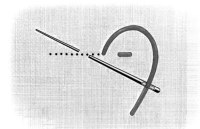

RUNNING STITCH

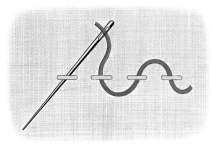

WHIPPED RUNNING STITCH

Appliqued placemat

You will need:

40 x 30cm hessian fabric
Felt
Wool
Sewing thread
Bodkin or large needle
Buttons, braid or lace
Scissors
Pins

1. Fringe the hessian mat by removing threads along each edge.

2. Cut out felt shapes to make a design. Pin felt pieces onto hessian.

3. Using sewing thread or wool and a bodkin or needle, stitch the felt pieces to the hessian. First knot the thread then bring the needle up through the fabric from the wrong side. To finish each thread length, take the needle through to the back of the fabric and make two small secure stitches on top of each other. Embroidery stitches can be used (see diagrams at left).

4. Stitch buttons, braid or lace onto the mat as desired.

Branch weaving

You will need:

String
Large dead branch
Weaving materials: fabric strips,
    wool, pantihose, feathers, leather
    scraps, rope, fleece, tinsel
Scissors

1. Wrap string around the branch in a random manner, knotting it on the main limb and wrapping it around the smaller branches.

2. Weave materials over and under the string. Add extra strands of string wherever necessary and continue until weaving is complete. Feathers and other small pieces can then be added into the weaving.

To display the weaving, suspend it from the ceiling or stand it in a plant pot.

◇Mesh stitching

You will need:

Orange or onion mesh bag
Coloured cardboard
Masking tape
Colourful yarn
Scissors

1. Adult. Cut the bag to give a flat piece of mesh fabric. Cut the cardboard to make a frame. Cut a piece from the inside of the cardboard; it could be an irregular shape, see picture.

2. Securely tape the mesh to the cardboard frame. Trim excess mesh.

3. Wrap a small piece of tape around the end of a yarn length (this makes the yarn end stiff enough to thread through the mesh). Using the coloured yarns, stitch patterns through the holes in the mesh.

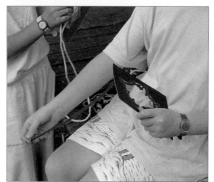

Mesh stitching makes an unusual wall or window hanging.

Puppets

Few crafts come to life as delightfully as a handcrafted puppet. They are entertaining, fun to make and educationally valuable. Puppets encourage creative play, promote interaction with play partners and help to develop social and communication skills. Shy children can communicate more easily through their puppet character in a pretend world. The puppets in this chapter are made by techniques ranging from papier mache to simple stitchery. Larger puppets are best tackled by a group of children. A good follow-up activity to a group project is to devise and perform a puppet play.

Broom puppet

You will need:

Lightweight cardboard
Broom or mop
3 dowel rods, each 90cm-long
Old long-sleeve shirt
Masking tape
Buttons, fringe, pipecleaners (for facial features)
2 pieces of cord or string (about half a metre long)
Paint
PVA glue
Scissors

1. Stand the broom or mop bristle-end up. Tape the small dowel across the broom handle below the broom to make a T shape. This will form the shoulders of the puppet.

2. Draw a face shape on cardboard large enough to fit over the broom. Tape the face to the broom handle so that the bristles or mop top stick out above the face like hair.

3. Glue on a cardboard shape for nose. Add button eyes, fringing for eyebrows, pipe cleaner ears and paint facial features as desired.

4. Dress the puppet in the shirt. Cut two hands from cardboard. Staple a hand and one end of a piece of cord to each sleeve cuff.

5. Tie one end of the cord to one of the remaining dowel rods. Repeat for other hand. Two children can move the puppet, one operating the centre rod and another operating the arm-control rods; however it's easier with three children, one on each rod.

Try making other faces to attach to the broom; have a different set of clothing for each character.

Sock puppet

You will need:

One sock
Thin black cardboard
Buttons (for eyes)
Felt fabric
Wool (optional)
Sewing thread and needle
PVA glue
Pins
Scissors

1. Cut a cardboard rectangle about 7cm x 20cm and curve the corners.

2. Slit the sock around the toe area. Fold the cardboard rectangle in half to form the inside of the mouth. Place the cardboard inside the slit of the sock, aligning the rounded edge with sock edge. Glue in place.

3. Decorate your puppet to create an animal or fantasy creature by stitching on felt shapes for body features and buttons for eyes.

 Bird puppet ✏️✏️✏️

You will need:

White fabric (twice as large as
  bird's head)
Crayon or pencil
Fabric or crepe paper strips, yellow
  and white
3 thick dowels or broom handles
Fibre filling or crumpled paper
Paint
Brushes
Sewing machine or stapler
Cord (twice the length of the
  desired wingspan plus 50cm)
Scissors

1. Draw a small reference diagram of a bird's head. Fold the white fabric in half and, using crayon, copy the shape on fabric. Cut out the bird's head through both layers of fabric.

2. Paint the bird's eyes, beak and topknot on one side of the bird's head and leave to dry. Paint the other side and allow to dry. Stitch or staple around the head, close to the edges, leaving the bottom of the neck open.

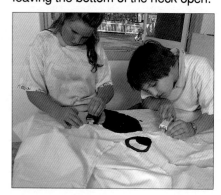

3. Stuff the head until it is half full. Push one dowel into the stuffing and continue filling around the dowel until the head is nearly full.

4. Pull the neck edge in around the pole. Tie the centre of the cord around the neck and the pole, securing the fabric edge.

5. Tie the ends of the cord to the remaining two dowels. Tie yellow and white fabric or crepe paper strips to the cords to form wings.

With one person holding each pole, flap the wings and "fly" the bird.

Cylinder puppet

OVER 6 YEARS

You will need:

Long cardboard cylinder
Cardboard scraps
Felt, pink and contrasting colours
Fabric scraps
Wool or raffia
Buttons
Fabric paint
Glue
Scissors

1. Using a child's hand as a guide, draw a three-fingered hand shape onto felt. Cut out the felt making the piece at least 3cm larger than the child's hand.

Make cylinder puppets based on characters from a favourite storybook and use the puppets to tell the story.

2. Cut the cardboard cylinder into three pieces; one 7cm-long and two 5cm-long. Glue two short pieces to the outer finger and thumb sections of the felt hand; these will make the puppet's hands. Glue the centre finger section inside the 7cm-long cylinder to make the puppet's head.

3. Cover the head cylinder with pink felt. Glue on a rolled felt strip for the puppet's nose. Cut out two hand shapes from pink felt and glue them inside the hand cylinders.

4. Cut legs and shoes from cardboard and cover in fabric or felt. Glue them onto the main felt piece.

5. Cut clothes from fabric scraps and wool. Use fabric paint, felt scraps and buttons for facial features. Make hair from wool or raffia and glue onto the head cylinder. The girl puppet's hair was made by taking a bundle of yarns and plaiting at each end, leaving an unplaited section in the centre. The boy's hair is raffia.

 # Box head puppet

You will need:

1 large cardboard box (head)
Scrap cardboard, cylinders and cones
Paper streamers
1.8m thick dowel (centre rod)
50cm thin dowel (shoulders)
Two thin 90cm dowels (arm control rods)
70cm cotton tape
Long-sleeve shirt
One pair of gloves
Fibre filling or crumpled paper
Paint
PVA glue
Thumb tacks
Paint brush
Masking tape
Scissors

1. Using scrap cardboard, cylinders or cones, make the puppet's nose, mouth, ears and eyes. We used empty film canisters for eyeballs and fringes of cardboard for eyelashes. Glue or tape these facial features onto the box-head, leaving the bottom of the box open.

2. Paint the head, emphasising the features with bright paint. Glue on paper streamers for hair.

3. Tape the shoulder dowel across and at right angles to the centre rod, about 40cm from one end of the rod.

4. Using a thumbtack, attach the 35cm lengths of tape to each end of the shoulder rod. Tape the central rod securely inside the box at the front side of the head, positioning the base of the head near the shoulder rod.

5. Dress the puppet in the shirt, threading the shoulder rods and arm tapes through the sleeves. Trim both arm tapes until they are the same length as the sleeves.

6. To make hands, stuff each glove with fibre filling or crumpled paper and staple these to the end of the arm tapes. Glue or stitch sleeves to the top of the hands. Tie arm control rods to the free ends of each tape.

Two or three people can operate this puppet. One person controls the central rod with that person's legs becoming the legs of the puppet. One or two people control the arm-rods.

Shadow puppet play ✎✏✎

You will need:

Wire coathangers
Cardboard
Crayon or pencil
Masking tape
Scissors
Plain light-coloured bed sheet
Light source (desk lamp, porta
   flood, etc.)

1. Adult. Straighten out a wire coathanger then bend the wire in half to make a long handle.

2. Using a crayon or pencil, draw an outline of an animal, person or creature on cardboard. Facial and body details are not needed. Inspiration for childrens' drawings can be provided by animal photographs or pictures.

3. Cut around the character and cut out eyes. Tape the character onto one end of the coat hanger. Wrap masking tape around the other end of the coathanger.

4. Make a screen by hanging the bed sheet over a rope or rods, or by fixing it at each corner.

5. Use the puppet between a light source and the fabric screen, while the audience looks on from the other side of the screen.

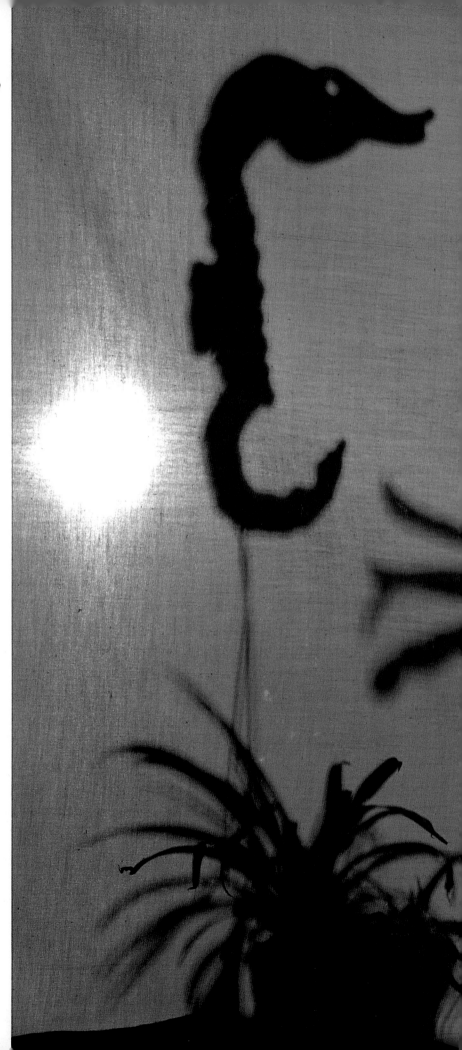

Jointed characters can be made by cutting and joining limbs with paper fasteners. To move the limbs simply attach a rod to each moving part.

Monster puppet

To make a dragon, add a strip of zigzag spines down this puppet's back and decorate the body fabric with scale shapes.

You will need:

Large foam block or small pieces glued together
Thin foam piece for teeth
3 metres of 115cm-wide calico
50cm red felt or fabric piece (for tongue)
Fabric strips, yarn, fringing
3 hoops (cane, plastic or 6 metres garden hose)

Ice cream sticks
Stanley knife or electric knife
Scissors
PVA glue
Stapler
Masking tape
Paint
Paintbrush
Scissors

1. Adult. Using scissors, stanley knife or electric knife, carve a head shape from the foam block. Cut chunks from the block to give the body a lumpy texture.

2. Adult. Carve a hollow to fit the child's head in the under section of the monster head. Glue or tie another piece of foam to form the mouth or cut an opening in the large block.

3. Cut a zigzag pattern from a thin foam piece to make teeth. Glue this piece to the inside of the mouth. Glue on foam pieces for eyes. Add ice-cream sticks for eyelashes. Ping pong balls could be used for eyeballs, if desired.

4. Paint the monster's head in suitable colours. Tie or glue the 50cm felt or fabric piece inside the mouth. Cut into shape for tongue.

5. Decorate the body by making small cuts in the calico and tying fabric strips or fringing through the cuts. Fabric strips can be plaited, have buttons tied on, or just left hanging. The body could also be decorated by painting.

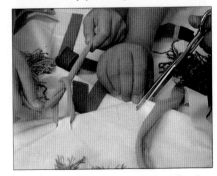

6. Adult. Cut hoops in half or, if using garden hose, cut 1 metre lengths and bend into a semi-circle.

7. Stitch half a hoop piece at regular intervals under the body fabric. The hoops shape the body and provide handholds for operators.

8. Tie, glue or stitch body fabric to the back of the head. Tie or stitch a piece of fringing at the back of the head for the mane or attach extra fabric strips or yarn.

To operate the monster, each child holds a hoop and one child stands underneath the head. The monster can be used at parades, festivals, school fetes or plays.

Glove puppet

You will need:

Plain, long or short glove
Fabric, felt and fur scraps, wool,
    buttons, beads or feathers (as
    desired)
PVA glue
Needle and thread
Scissors

1. Ask children about the type of glove puppet they would like to make. Animal pictures may provide inspiration and ideas; our puppet was created from a picture of a panda.

2. Glue or stitch felt, wool, fur or buttons onto the glove to create the puppet you desire.

Each finger could be a different puppet character or the whole glove could be one puppet. The puppet character could be human or animal; real or imaginary.

Windsock

You will need:

4 metres of lightweight fabric
Fabric scraps, bright colours
Broom handle or thick dowel
Plastic, cane or wire hoop
4 metres strong cord
Sewing machine (or stapler)
PVA or fabric glue
Needle and thread
Stapler
Scissors

1. Fold the fabric in half across the width to give a 2 metre length. Draw the windsock shape onto the fabric. A shape that will make a wind tunnel, open at both ends, is needed. A fish shape works well. Cut out the windsock shape through both layers of fabric.

2. Decorate the outside of the windsock with paint, fabric scraps, sequins or braid. We cut scallops and spots from fabric scraps and glued them to the main fabric.

3. With right sides together, stitch or staple the side seams of the windsock, leaving both top and bottom ends unstitched. Turn through to right side. Staple paper streamers to the bottom edge of the windsock.

4. Securely stitch a hoop around the mouth of the windsock. If the hoop is too large, cut a piece out and rejoin the hoop with tape. Attach cord at three places around the hoop and onto the rod.

To fly the windsock attach it to a post outdoors or play with it like a hand-held kite.

Recycled Fun

Give new life to household junk; turn it into inexpensive, creative craft. Only two rules apply; recognise the value of useful "garbage" before it is thrown away, and, use our projects as guidelines only, encouraging the child's own imagination and creativity.

◆8◆ White poodle ✏️➡️✏️

You will need:

Thin white plastic shopping bags
Rectangular polystyrene piece
Old ballpoint pen
Thick white sock
Newspaper
2 pairs of white pantihose or
    stockings
4 plastic lids, such as those from
    margarine containers
2 plastic teaspoons
Pink fabric scrap (for tongue)
Adhesive tape
Rubber bands
Black felt pen
Fishing line
Stiff black plastic, such as a soft
    drink bottle base
Star stickers
Glue
Scissors

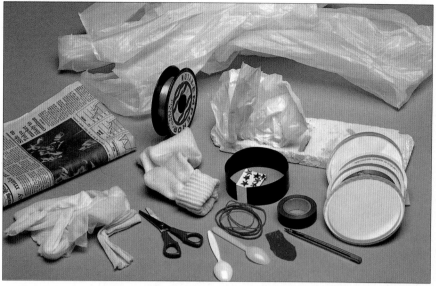

1. Cut the bottom seam and handles off each shopping bag. Cut the sides of the bag so that you have two pieces. To make the poodle's body, place the polystyrene piece on a flat surface and push the plastic bags into the polystyrene piece using a ballpoint pen. Continue until one side of the polystyrene piece is well covered. This will be the top side of the poodle.

2. Trim the plastic bag ends so that the coat is approximately the same length all over, but long enough to cover the edges of the polystyrene.

3. Make a nose at the toe of the sock by holding a couple of tucks with a rubber band. Colour the nose black or pink with a felt pen.

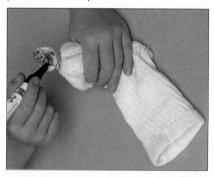

4. Stuff the foot of the sock firmly with balls of newspaper. Make the poodle's topknot by putting a rubber band around the heel of the sock. Stuff more newspaper into the leg of the sock.

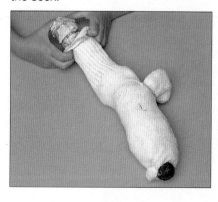

5. Draw eyes on plastic teaspoons with a felt pen. Slip the spoon handles under the rubber band which holds the topknot. Cut a long strip of a plastic bag to make ears. Slip the centre of the plastic strip under the rubber band at the topknot.

Cut a strip of pink fabric and slip it under the rubber band at the nose. Trim the tongue to the right length and shape then secure with glue.

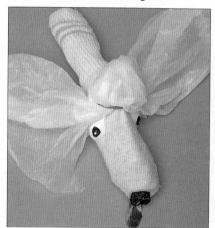

6. Place a rubber band over each end of the polystyrene body piece. Tie the sock onto the band at one end of the body. Tie a roughly fringed plastic bag around base of neck to hide where it joins the body.

7. Cut a strip of black plastic for the collar. Decorate with star stickers and put around the poodle's neck. Secure with tape if necessary.

8. Cut the legs off the pantihose. Tie pantihose legs through the rubber bands on the poodle's body so that a leg hangs down on each corner of the body. Cut feet off pantyhose.

9. Push a plastic lid inside each leg and knot the pantyhose leg under the lid. Hold the lid in place with tape, as pictured.

10. Tie a length of fishing line to top of head and to rubber band at other end of body. Hold fishing line to make the poodle walk, sit or stand.

Use different coloured bags to make a more colourful puppy.

Hamburger puppet

You will need:

1 takeaway hamburger pack
1 pair of coloured tights
2 plastic teaspoons
1 foil packet
Stickers (for nostrils)
1 plastic bread-wrapper tie
1 milk carton
Rubber bands
Felt pen
Tape
Scissors

1. Put two strong rubber bands over the whole of the hamburger pack, near the hinge. The puppet's mouth will open and close when fingers and thumb are placed through each band from behind the hinge of the pack.

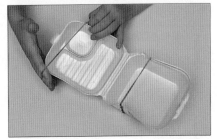

2. Pull tights over the hamburger pack, from behind the hinge, placing the waist inside the pack. Pull a strong rubber band over the tights and across hinge of the hamburger pack. Legs should hang at each side of the hinge.

Cut the tights behind the hinge to make an opening for your hand.

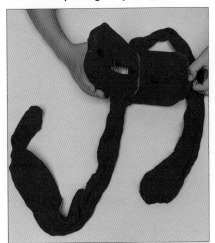

3. Adult. Make slits at top and front edge of the hamburger pack and push the handles of teaspoons through from top to front edge to make eyes and tusks.

4. Cut the foil packet in a fringe leaving strips attached at one end.

5. Roll up the foil packet and tape in a roll at the intact end. **Adult.** Make a small slit in the back of the hamburger pack and push the taped end of the packet through the slit to make hair.

6. Place stickers on spoons for eyes or draw with a felt pen. A bread tie hooked around tights at the front edge makes the nose. Draw nostrils on the bread tie with a felt pen.

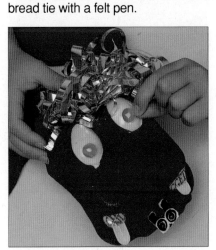

7. Legs of tights make the puppet's legs. Tie knots halfway down legs for knees. Cut some feet from the milk carton. Draw claws with a felt pen. **Adult.** Make a small slit in the foot and push tights through. Knot tights under the foot to secure them.

Cup clown

You will need:

1 large paper cup
Paper serviette or tissue paper
Coloured stickers
Stapler
Scissors

1. Cut cup from rim to base in five strips. Cut a piece off the rim end of one strip. The short strip remaining attached to the cup will be the clown's head. Trim the strips on each side of the head to make arms.

2. Trim the cut off piece into a triangular shape to make a hat.

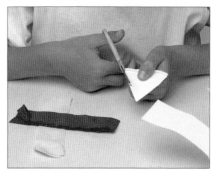

3. Cut a piece of the serviette or tissue paper into strips.

4. Staple paper strips to the top of the head to make hair. Staple triangular hat over hair.

5. Cut wide strips of serviette or tissue paper for the frills around cuffs and neck. Gather strips of paper and staple them onto the clown at the neck, wrists and ankles to make frills. Place a row of stickers down the front of the clown's body and hat. Add other stickers for eyes and mouth.

Hang the clown from a string or bend his knees to make him sit.

Wriggling snake

You will need:

Plastic plate
Plastic cup
Stickers
Thread
Felt pen
Adhesive tape or stapler
Scissors

1. Cut a strip from around the rim of a plastic plate until the plate is about half the original size. Keeping the strip attached, cut a head shape from the centre of the plate.

2. Trim the snake's neck and head until you are happy with the shape. Add stickers for eyes and draw the mouth with a felt pen. Cut a tongue-shape from the plastic cup. Tape or staple it onto the head.

Tie a thread around the neck of the snake. Use it to hang the snake or make him wriggle. If the snake's head won't sit flat it can be cut off and re-attached with staples or tape.

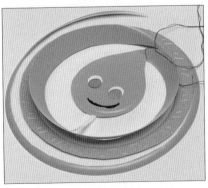

Using a felt pen, decorate the snake's body with diamonds or stripes.

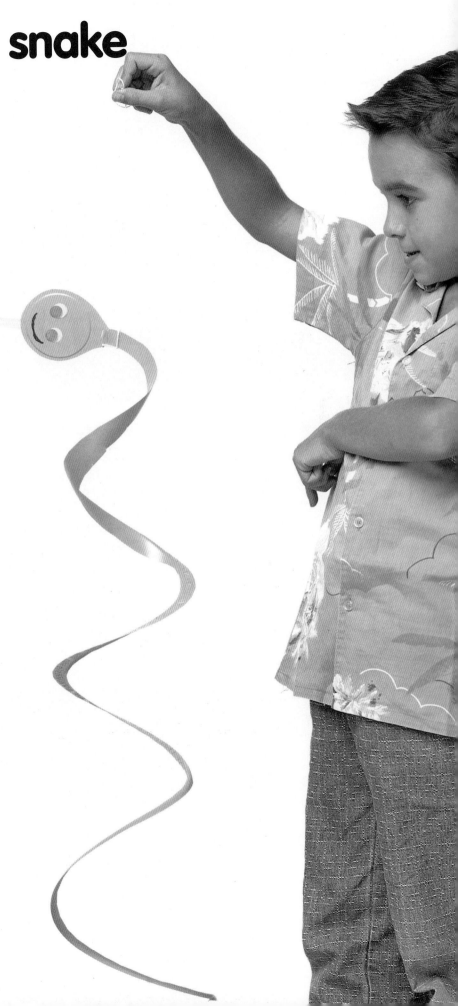

◆ Cuppa snake ✏️🖊️✏️

OVER 5 YEARS

You will need:

Pantihose leg or a stocking
Coloured plastic cups
Newspaper
2 coloured plastic plates
Paper fasteners
Ballpoint pen
Scissors
Fishing line (optional)
Stick (optional)

1. Using a ballpoint pen, punch a hole in the base of each cup. Thread cups onto the pantihose leg through the hole in the cup base. To space cups apart, place a ball of newspaper into each cup after it is threaded.

2. For the head, cut the rim off a plastic plate and punch two holes in eye positions. Punch a large third hole at the edge of the plate, above and between the eyes and thread the end of the pantihose through this hole. Thread the pantihose end through the base of another cup which will be a hat. Secure the head and hat with a knot in the pantihose.

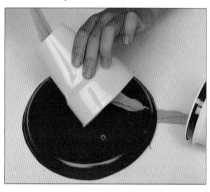

3. Cut the base off two plastic cups to make eyes. Attach each base to the plate with paper fasteners. Cut a strip of plastic shaped like a tongue. Punch a hole and attach it to the plate using a paper fastener.

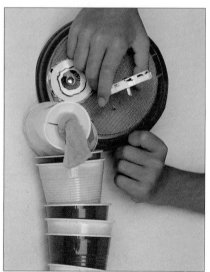

4. Cut a triangular plastic piece for the tail tip. Punch a hole through the wide end of the plastic piece and thread it onto the end of the snake's tail. Knot the pantihose at the tail end to secure the tail.

To make a moving snake, punch holes at three points along the length of the snake and attach some fishing line, tie the other end of the fishing line to the stick. Shake the stick and the snake will wriggle.

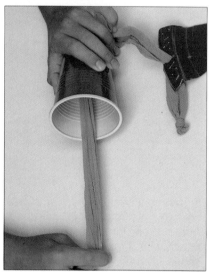

Attach fishing line to the snake and hang it from the ceiling of the child's room.

Hang the starfish and jellyfish near a window so the light shines through them.

Sea creatures

You will need:

1 round clear plastic container and lid, such as a take-away food container
Tissue paper
Stickers
Felt pen
Thread
Glue
Stapler
Scissors

STARFISH

1. Cut the side of the plastic container from the base. Cut five triangles from the side piece of the container.

2. Staple the five triangles around the base of the container to make the starfish.

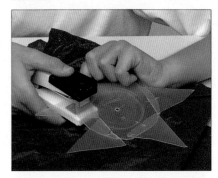

3. Cover the starfish in glue. Lay the starfish onto tissue paper and bunch up the paper to give a bumpy texture.
Fold and glue the overhanging paper onto the starfish body so the outline shows clearly. Add more paper if you want a thicker starfish.

4. When the glue is dry, staple a hanging thread to the starfish. Add stickers for eyes and draw details with a felt pen.

JELLYFISH

1. Cut the plastic lid in half.

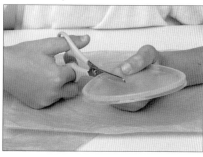

2. Glue the lid halves together as pictured above.

3. Cover the lid with glue on both sides. Cut or tear a large rectangle of tissue paper. Lay the lid in the centre of the paper with the curved side of the lid next to the fold of the paper. Fold the tissue paper over the lid as pictured.

4. Glue and fold the paper around the curved edge of the lid. Bunch and gather the paper to give a bumpy texture. Leave about 10cm of paper hanging free from the straight edge of the lid.

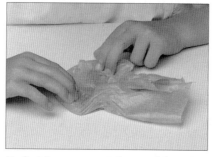

5. Cut the paper at the straight edge of the lid into strips to make tendrils. Attach a thread for hanging. Add stickers for eyes and draw details with a felt pen.

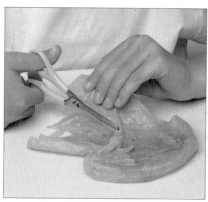

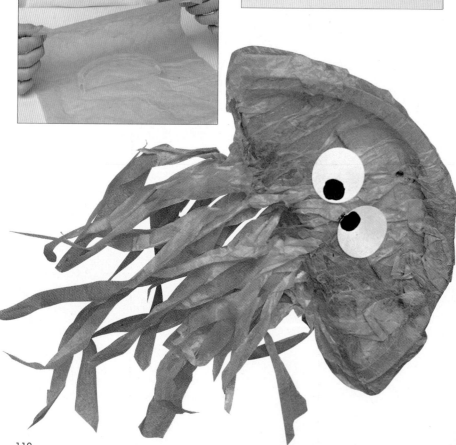

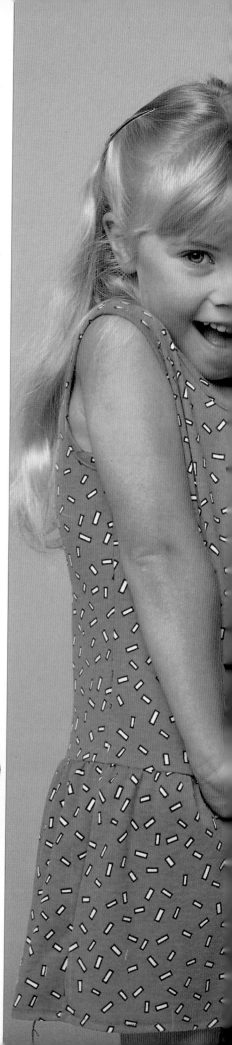

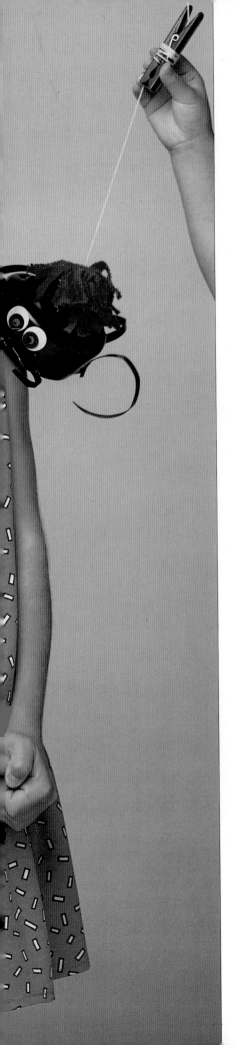

Spider

You will need:

Soft drink bottle base
Red fabric scrap
Thread
Ballpoint pen
Stickers
Felt pen
Glue
Stapler
Scissors

1. Cut off a strip from around the rim of the bottle base.

2. Cut the strip into eight thin legs.

3. Adult. Soften the remaining base piece in hot water. Push the bottom out to make it rounded.

4. Adult assistance. Staple the legs around the edge of the base, positioning them curving out from the body.

5. Cut the fabric scrap into strips and tie in a bundle with thread. Punch two holes in the base with a ballpoint pen. Insert a length of thread through the holes. Tie the bundle of fabric strips over the holes to make hair.

6. Add stickers for eyes. Draw details in felt pen.

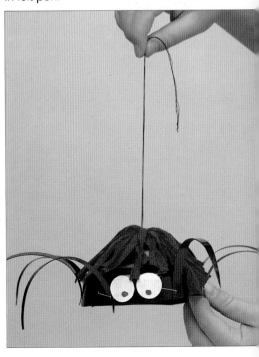

119

Fish kite

OVER 5 YEARS

You will need:

Foil liner from orange juice or wine
  cask
Small plastic plate
Coloured plastic shopping bag
2 plastic cups
Paper fasteners
Felt pen
String
Stapler
Scissors

1. Adult assistance. Cut the ends off
the foil liner. Wash out the liner and
remove plastic tap. This will be the tail
end of the fish kite. Cut the rim off a
plastic plate. Staple the plate rim
around the liner opening, at the mouth
end. The plate will form the mouth.

2. Fold two or three tucks into the tail
end of the liner. Cut the plastic bag
into a fringe, leaving the strips of the
fringe attached at one end. Staple a
large piece of the fringe to the tail end,
reserving some fringe for the fins.

3. Tape small pieces of fringe to the
fish body for fins.

4. Cut the round base from two plastic cups for eyes (or use the remains
of the plastic plate). Make a hole in the
centre of each cup base and attach
eyes to fish using paper fasteners.
Draw details with felt pen.

5. Adult. Punch a hole and thread a
string through the top of the mouth.

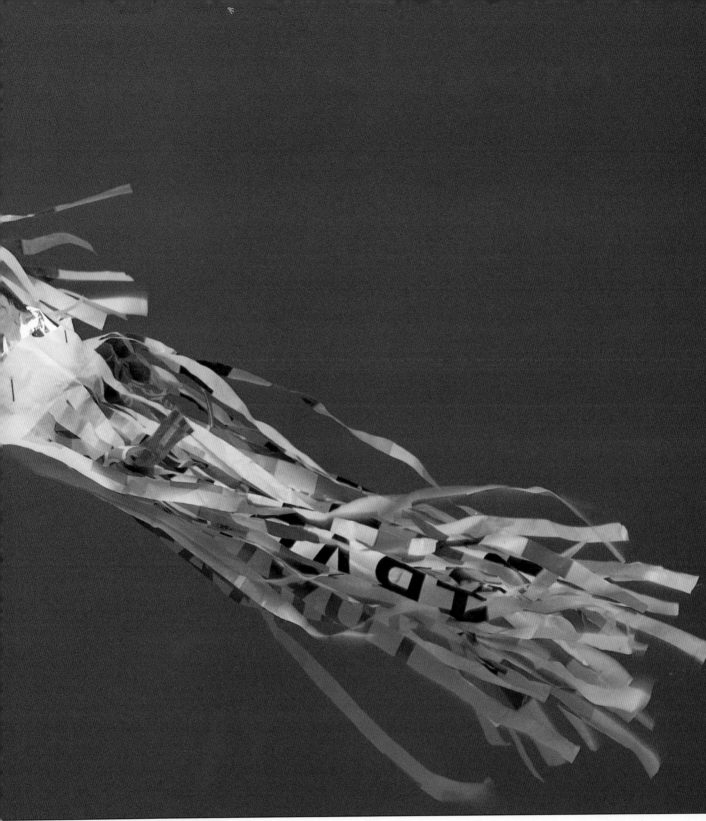

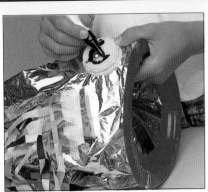

*Use the fish as a kite
or a mobile.*

Hopping rabbit finger puppet

You will need:

1 small plastic container, such as a yoghurt container
Coloured cotton wool balls
1 plastic lid, such as a margarine container lid
Crayon (optional)
Glue
Felt pen
Scissors

1. Adult. Cut two holes in one side of the yoghurt container. They should be large enough for a child to put their fingers through.

2. Glue cotton wool balls around the sides of the container.

3. Adult. Cut two slits at the bottom edge of the container on the opposite side of the two finger-holes.

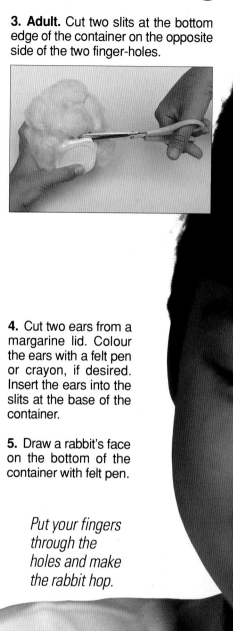

4. Cut two ears from a margarine lid. Colour the ears with a felt pen or crayon, if desired. Insert the ears into the slits at the base of the container.

5. Draw a rabbit's face on the bottom of the container with felt pen.

Put your fingers through the holes and make the rabbit hop.

Plastic cup flowers

OVER 5 YEARS

You will need:

Coloured plastic cups
Tissue paper or paper serviette
Drinking straws with bendable joint
Adhesive tape
Stickers
Glue
Scissors
Vase, pot or branch

Variation: Cut individual petal shapes from plastic cup or plate and tape together at the flower centre. Use the base of a second cup for the centre and fill with coloured cotton wool, or use stickers to decorate the centre.

1. Cut the rim off a plastic cup. Fringe the cup from rim almost to the base, without breaking off the pieces. One cup can be glued inside another to make extra petals, if desired.

3. Trim a drinking straw to size desired, tape to back of the flower for the stem. Arrange flowers in a vase, pot or tape to a branch for display.

2. Gently bend the petals back. Crumple a piece of tissue paper or paper serviette and glue it into the base of the cup. Crumple tiny balls of a contrasting colour paper and glue them around the edge of the first paper centre.

Net clown

OVER 6 YEARS

You will need:

2 small net onion bags
2 patty pan papers
Lid from detergent bottle
Paper serviette
Coloured plastic plate
Star stickers
String
Felt pen
Stapler
Adhesive tape
Scissors

1. Tie one net bag in the middle with string. This will make two legs.

2. Cut the other bag in half to make arms and tunic. Fold each piece in half and place one on each side of the legs. The cut edge will be the tunic frill.

3. Adult assistance. Tape around the fold and top of legs to make clown's neck, leaving the string ends free at the neck.

4. Adult. Make a small hole in the centre of two patty papers, turn them upside down and thread strings through the hole in the papers then through the detergent bottle lid.

5. Cut the cap off the lid. Cut thin strips of serviette and tie them tightly in a bundle with the string, making a mop of hair.

6. Cut feet from a plastic plate and staple them to the bottom of each leg.

7. Draw on the clown's face with a felt pen. Decorate the tunic frill with star stickers.

Elephant

You will need:

1 (2 litre) juice or cordial container
2 (250ml) juice pack cartons (optional)
2 pairs of pantihose or tights
Newspaper
2 oval paper plates
Rim of large ice-cream container
Small piece of cardboard
Paint and paintbrush, or can of spray paint
Paper serviettes
Paper fasteners
Felt pen
String
Glue
Adhesive tape
Scissors

1. Adult. Cut the base off the juice container.

2. Tape a juice pack to the front and back neck of the juice container. If you do not have the juice packs, simply proceed with Step 3; the newspaper will pad out the head shape.

3. Cut off one leg from each pair of pantihose. Discard the cut-off legs. Fill one leg of pantihose with balls of crumpled newspaper until long enough for the elephant's trunk.

4. Place the neck end of the juice bottle into the pantihose and pack more newspaper around the bottle to shape the head, as pictured.

5. Pull the waist of the pantihose over and into the back of the juice container. Pull the second pair of pantihose over the trunk and pull the waist into the juice container. Allow the pantihose to wrinkle, like elephant's skin.

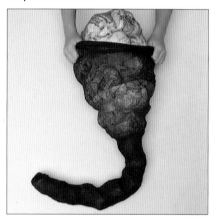

6. Cut one side off each paper plate. **Adult assistance.** Make three holes along the cut edge. Attach plates to each side of the elephant's head using paper fasteners through pantihose and holes in the plate.

7. Adult assistance. Paint the elephant. with a paintbrush or a spray can. Leave to dry.

8. Cut two large ovals for eyes from cardboard. Glue eyes on and draw details with felt pen. Cut serviettes into strips and tie tightly in a bundle with string. Make two holes in the top of head and tie hair on.

9. Adult assistance. Cut one side off the rim of the ice-cream container so three sides remain. Punch a hole underneath the elephant's trunk, from one side to the other. Insert ice-cream container strip through the holes to form tusks.

Insert your arm into the elephant's head and make his trunk swing.

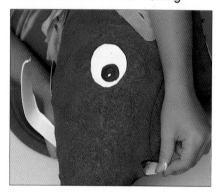

Design other animal faces to make using this method.

Index

A,B

Appliqued placemat	85
Balloon prints	32
Binoculars	63
Bird puppet	92
Block print stamp	31
Box head puppet	96
Branch weaving	86
Broom puppet	90
Brush discovery painting	14

C,D

Chicken wire mask	76
Coloured ice melts	48
Cone hats	70
CONSTRUCTION AND COLLAGE	56
- Coloured glasses	62
- Mixed material collage	58
- Paper collage	64
- Polystyrene sculpture	60
- Wire sculpture	61
Crayon screen print	36
Cup clown	112
Cuppa snake	114
Cylinder puppet	94
Dip and dye	40
Drinking straw weaving	84
DYEING	38
- Dip and dye	40
- Multi-coloured tie dyeing	42
- Peg dyeing	44
- Reverse dip and dye	45
- Reverse tie-dyeing	43

E,F,G

Elephant	126
Fingerpainting	6
Fingerpainting prints	8
Fish kite	120
Floating and sinking	52
Foam prints	24
Glove puppet	103
Goop	54
Guidelines	2

H,J, K

Hamburger puppet	110
Hessian weaving	81
Hopping rabbit finger puppet	122
Jellyfish	118
Kitchen gadget printing	35

M,N,O

Magic painting	19
MASKS AND HATS	66
- Chicken wire mask	76
- Cone hats	70
- New faces	68
- Papier mache mask with clay mould	71
- Party hats	73
- Plaster bandage mask	74
Mesh dab-prints	25
Mesh stitching	87
Mix and mess	52
Mixed material collage	58
Mono-printed doll	27
Monster painting	20
Monster puppet	100
Multi-coloured tie dyeing	42
Nature weaving	80
Net clown	125
New faces	68
Opera glasses	62

P

PAINTING	4
- Brush discovery painting	14
- Fingerpainting	6
- Magic painting	19
- Monster painting	20
- Roller painting	18
- Sponge painting	16
- Spray paint mural	11
- String and fibre painting	15
Paper collage	64
Papier mache mask with clay mould	71
Party hats	73
Peg dyeing	44
Plaster bandage mask	74
Plastic cup flowers	123
Polystyrene sculpture	60
PRINTING	22
- Balloon prints	32
- Block print stamp	31
- Crayon screen print	36
- Foam prints	24
- Kitchen gadget printing	35
- Mesh dab-prints	25
- Mono-printed doll	27
- Roller printing	34
- Spool printing	30
- Tennis ball prints	26
PUPPETS	88
-Bird puppet	92
- Box head puppet	96
- Broom puppet	90
- Cylinder puppet	94
- Glove puppet	103
- Monster puppet	100
- Mono-printed doll	27
- Shadow puppet play	98
- Sock puppet	91
- Windsock	104

R

RECYCLED FUN	106
- Cup clown	112
- Cuppa snake	114
- Elephant	126
- Fish kite	120
- Hamburger puppet	110
- Hopping rabbit finger puppet	122
- Net clown	125
- Plastic cup flowers	123
- Sea creatures	116
- Spider	119
- White poodle	108
- Wriggling snake	113
Reverse dip and dye	45
Reverse tie-dyeing	43
Roller painting	18
Roller printing	34

S

Sea creatures	116
Scraper prints	8
Shadow puppet play	98
Slime	50
Sock puppet	91
Spider	119
Sponge painting	16
Spool printing	30
Spray paint mural	11
Starfish	117
String and fibre painting	15

T

Telescope	63
Tennis ball prints	26
Texture rubbing	49
TOUCH AND FEEL	46
- Coloured ice melts	48
- Floating and sinking	52
- Goop	54
- Mix and mess	52
- Slime	50
- Texture rubbing	49

W

WEAVING AND STITCHING	78
- Appliqued placemat	85
- Branch weaving	86
- Drinking straw weaving	84
- Hessian weaving	81
- Mesh stitching	87
- Nature weaving	80
- Weaving on a box loom	82
- Weaving on wire	83
Weaving on a box loom	82
Weaving on wire	83
White poodle	108
Windsock	104
Wire sculpture	61
Wriggling snake	113